YOU ARE UNSTOPPABLE!

Unleash Your Inspired Life

Thomas S. Narofsky

Copyright © 2014 Thomas S. Narofsky
Narofsky Consulting Group, LLC
Papillion, NE

The Narofsky Consulting Group is committed to building leaders that are ready to lead in an uncertain and ambiguous world with integrity, values, and character.

NarofskyConsultingGroup@gmail.com

Cover design by KJ Paperie

All rights reserved

Disclaimer: There is no official endorsement of this book or the material contained herein by the Department of Defense, United States Strategic Command, or the United States Air Force. The thoughts, opinions, anecdotes, Inspire or Retire Theorem, the F(X) Leadership concepts, the F(X) FORGE Process, the 6P Focus, and the Unstoppable Discovery Process and Unstoppable Life Models are the intellectual property of the Narofsky Consulting Group. The processes and models contained herein may not be suitable for every situation.

Title ID: 4530217
ISBN-13: 978-1493798032

DEDICATION

This book is dedicated to our grandchildren, Titus and Eliza Belle, and Kyrie Grace, our future grandchildren, and their children. Believe in God, believe in yourselves, and have faith that you are unstoppable!

"Do not let your fire go out, spark by irreplaceable spark in the hopeless swamps of the not-quite, the not-yet, and the not-at-all. Do not let the hero in your soul perish in lonely frustration for the life you deserved and have never been able to reach. The world you desire can be won. It exists.. it is real.. it is possible...it's yours."

Ayn Rand

CONTENTS

Acknowledgments

Preface

Introduction

Chapter 1   A CALL TO UNSTOPPABLE ACTION

Your Life is Unstoppable	Pg. 2
Be Inspired	Pg. 4
Live Greatly	Pg. 5
Change Yourself	Pg. 6
Change Your Mindset	Pg. 7
Take Charge of Your Life	Pg. 8
You are Responsible	Pg. 10
You are Accountable	Pg. 11
Never Give Up	Pg. 12
Take Action	Pg. 13
The First Law: Wake Up!	Pg. 14
Get Out of You C.O.M.F.O.R.T Zone	Pg. 15
The Second Law: Get Moving!	Pg. 17
Be the Change Agent of Your Life	Pg. 18

	The Third Law: No Pressure No Diamonds	Pg. 20
	Challenges will Forge You	Pg. 21
	Reflection Time	Pg. 25
Chapter 2	IN THE BEGINNING….	
	It All Begins with a Choice	Pg. 29
	The FORGE Discovery Process	Pg. 30
	Choices Determine Your Destiny	Pg. 33
	Kinetic Effects	Pg. 36
	Create Your Timeline	Pg. 38
	Reflection Time	Pg. 41
Chapter 3	SELF-LEADRSHIP IS THE KEY	
	A Great Way of Life	Pg. 45
	A Disciplined Approach	Pg. 48
	The Unstoppable Model	Pg. 52
	The Inner Core	Pg. 53
	The Outer Rings	Pg. 55
	Personal Insight	Pg. 56
	Personal Mastery	Pg. 57
	Eight Disciplines of Self-Development	Pg.59

	Eight Life Qualities	Pg. 62
	Reflection Time	Pg. 65
Chapter 4	THE INNER CORE:THE REAL YOU	
	Discover Your True Self	Pg. 69
	A Focused Life	Pg. 72
	Strategic Clarity	Pg. 77
	Life is a Journey	Pg. 78
	My Journey	Pg. 79
	Soul Searching	Pg. 81
	The Influence of the Inner Core	Pg. 83
	My #1 Core Value	Pg. 84
	Character	Pg. 85
	Reflection Time	Pg. 90
Chapter 5	UNSHAKEABLE LIFE PURPOSE	
	Here on Purpose	Pg. 94
	My Purpose	Pg. 96
	Discover Your Purpose	Pg. 96
	L.I.F.E.P.U.R.P.O.S.E.	Pg. 98
	Life Strategy	Pg. 103

	Envision Your Future	Pg. 104
	Visualization	Pg. 105
	Vision and Mission Statement	Pg. 107
	Reflection Time	Pg. 110
Chapter 6	THE OUTER RINGS: THE DEEP DIVE	
	Create a Masterpiece	Pg. 114
	Forge Ahead or Fall Behind	Pg. 115
	The FORGE Process	Pg. 117
	Goals, Objectives, and Actions	Pg. 123
	S.M.A.R2.T. Goals.	Pg. 126
	Eight Disciplines of Goal Setting	Pg. 129
	Reflection Time	Pg. 132
Chapter 7	YOU REAP WHAT YOU SOW	
	The Parable of the Farmer and Life	Pg. 136
	Unstoppable Life Matrix	Pg. 141
	The Unstoppable Quadrants	Pg. 142
	Living in Quadrant 4!	Pg. 144
	Develop and Grow Yourself	Pg. 145
	The Triad of Transformational Growth	Pg. 146

	The Enduring Learning Model	Pg. 148
	Deliberate Learning	Pg. 150
	Pathways to Developing Yourself	Pg. 153
	Reflection Time	Pg. 154
Chapter 8	A DISCIPLINED MIND	
	Thirty-Six Hours	Pg. 158
	A Changed Mind	Pg. 160
	PC3	Pg. 161
	The P4R Mind	Pg. 163
	The Positive Mind	Pg. 167
	Positive Mindset	Pg. 170
	A Warrior Focused Mind	Pg. 172
	Thinking Tactics	Pg. 174
	Improvise, Adapt, Overcome	Pg. 174
	Reframe, Rethink, Reinvent	Pg. 176
	Effects Mindset	Pg. 178
	The Outcomes Mindset	Pg. 180
	Fearless Focus	Pg. 182
	Reflection Time	Pg. 184

Chapter 9	LIVING LIFE UNSTOPPABLE	
	Unstoppable Attitude	Pg. 188
	The Unstoppable-Centered Life	Pg. 190
	The Power Cycle	Pg. 192
	Power #1: Believe in Yourself	Pg. 194
	Power #2: Courage and Confidence	Pg. 195
	Power #3: Resiliency	Pg. 201
	Power #4: Trust, Respect, and Integrity	Pg. 207
	Power #5: Humor and Humility	Pg. 208
	Power #6: Forgiveness and Grace	Pg. 209
	Power #7: Hope	Pg. 211
	Reflection Time	Pg. 213
Chapter 10	THE UNSTOPPABLE LIFE	
	My Grandfather	Pg. 217
	Unstoppable Life Effects	Pg. 218
	Fight The Good Fight	Pg. 224
	Living Your Unstoppable Legacy	Pg. 225
	An Unstoppable Declaration	Pg. 227
	Reflection Time	Pg. 233

You are Unstoppable!

Conclusion	Pg. 236
Living Life Unstoppable	Pg. 237
Living Your L.I.F.E on Mission	Pg. 241
What is Your Story	Pg. 244
Leaving a Legacy	Pg. 247
When do You Begin	Pg. 251
About the Author	Pg. 252

ACKNOWLEDGMENTS

To my Wife, Dorene Narofsky, whose proofreading, editing and positive support made this book a reality. Your encouragement, patience, and insight made this book possible. I love you today, tomorrow, and always.

To my Sons, Timothy, Joshua, and Jacob, and Daughters-in-Law, Rebekah, and Karis for your encouragement with the writing of my second book in a year. I am blessed to have you as a family.

PREFACE

The genesis of this book comes from my wounded warrior visits to Brooks Army Medical Center (BAMC) in 2006 prior to my yearlong deployment to the Middle East. While visiting the prosthetics lab I took the opportunity to talk to several Soldiers and Airmen to see how they were coping with their lives. What one young Soldier said during my visit made a lasting impact on me and gave me insight about resilience, perseverance, and passion for life.

During the visit, I had the chance to visit with a young Soldier who had lost a leg, an arm, and had burns to over 30% of his body during an IED explosion that killed two fellow Soldiers. When I first entered the lab, he was sitting at a table learning how to adjust and repair his leg in the same fashion he learned to field strip his rifle. This was part of his amputee rehabilitation and reintegration development. As he worked, we talked about how his life had changed and how he was coping with the changes. He said:

> Chief, I used to work out every day in the gym in order to keep myself fit and ready for the Army and life in general. I thought I was strong enough to handle whatever life could throw at me. I was wrong. The loss of my limbs crushed me and I immediately felt lost and depressed. I was very angry and mad at life. To be honest I did not want to go on.
>
> It was not until I arrived at Brooks that I started looking at life differently. After several counseling sessions, rehabilitation therapy, and being around other wounded warriors I realized how much life I still had in me. I learned how to fight for my life again. Today, I am stronger than I first thought I was. It is

not my physical strength I rely on now to get me through, it is my faith, my inner strength, and my belief in myself that makes go on each day.

I am stronger because I believe in myself and know I can do anything I want to do despite losing my arm and leg. I plan to live my life to its fullest each day.

His statement of clarity is powerful. He is stronger now than before he went to Iraq is poignant even today. In my opinion, he is unstoppable because he believes he can do anything through his faith and his faith in himself. Through his faith, he found hope again. When he found hope, he loved his life again. When he loved his life again he believed in himself and his life.

He is living an unstoppable life because he refuses to give up on himself, his dreams, and his aspirations. Life pushed in on him and he pushed back even harder and now is stronger. He is unstoppable because he has clarity of purpose and intentional clarity of his life.

His story of perseverance, positive outlook, and determined resiliency inspired me then and continues to inspire me. Despite his life changing injuries, he changed his life and his outlook on life. He chose to live each day intentionally and to its fullest.

You have a choice each day. You can choose to believe in who you are and live life to its fullest, or you can chose to run and hide from who you are and live unfulfilled. Your life takes on whatever meaning you give it. When you shift your daily focus and choices, and intentions, there is no limit on what your life can become.

You can choose to believe in your talents, gifts, capabilities, and abilities and accomplish great things, or you cannot believe in your ability and live a life of regret. You can choose to believe in your dreams and aspirations and make them become your reality, or you can choose to let you dreams remain a dream.

Whatever you believe in, you must put action to that belief. Just like the young Solider, you have to believe then apply the actions you need to make the belief your reality. You have to believe you can lead an unstoppable life and then apply the actions you need to realize an unstoppable life.

I believe we were created for a purpose. I believe each of us is here not by mistake, but by design. I believe each of us is here on this planet we call Earth on purpose and for a purpose. It is why I believe we are unstoppable. We were meant to live courageous and bold lives and not lives of mediocrity. However, we have to live our lives actively and on purpose each day to be unstoppable.

I BELIEVE YOU ARE UNSTOPPABLE!

THOMAS S. NAROFSKY

INTRODUCTION

"The dogmas of the quiet past are inadequate to the stormy present. The occasion is piled high with difficulty, and we must rise with the occasion. As our case is new, so we must think anew and act anew. We must disenthrall ourselves, and then we shall save our country."
Abraham Lincoln

If you have picked up my book, chances are you are here because you are an explorer, a discoverer, a seeker of knowledge wanting to learn more about who you are and what you can become. As an explorer you believe that life is a journey, an expedition, and adventure and you are not happy with the just being part of the status quo. You seek to continuously improve, change, and reinvent your life.

No matter the reason, you are here with the book in your hand ready to unlock your Unstoppable Life and Unleash your Inspired Life. The Unstoppable Personal Development System contains several models and processes that I have derived from my personal experiences, leadership development, and life opportunities.

My passion for self-development was fueled very early in my career by great leaders who encouraged, molded, and inspired me to achieve more than I thought I could. They invested time and guided me through a solid plan of personal and leadership development to hone and build my life.

This book is about you and your journey to be the best person and leader that you are meant to be. It's intended to help you discover and identify who you are, and why you came here to be a part of this World.

I BELIEVE YOU ARE UNSTOPPABLE!

This book is designed to make you intentionally think about your life and how you are developing yourself and living your life.

Your life is a sum total of the decisions, choices, and actions you have taken so far in your life. However, in reality it is only a sliver of what is in the realm of possible for your life.

Hidden deep within you is an unstoppable life waiting to emerge. You are an unstoppable person, wonderfully made, and born to thrive each day not merely survive.

However, if you are like most skeptical people, you do not completely grab hold of this concept. Then this book is a challenge to you and how you look at your life and how you are developing yourself. Even if you do not believe it yet, I believe that You Are Unstoppable!

Your Life is Your Message

Each day you live, you write a page in your life story. Each year you live, you add another chapter to your life story. Everything you say and do in your life adds to your life story. Your life story is your message to the world. What will your life story say about you? What will your message tell the world?

Will your message tell of a great odyssey like Odysseus had or will it tell a great tale of overcoming the odds like Earnest Shackleton? Will your message tell the world you lived an unstoppable life or will it tell a tale of mediocrity and a tale of an unlived life?

The truth is that you get to choose what your message will say because you get to write the storyline. Maybe you have been living uneventfully and maybe the message is not telling the story you want the world to read and hear. If that is true, then you can choose TODAY to write a new page in your unstoppable life. Stop for a moment and think about what you want your life to become.

Think about what you want your message to be. Think about the difference, the significance, the impact, and the inspiration your message can bring to others. What will your life message say to the world?

It begins with your how you choose to live you day. How do you wake up each morning? When was the last time you woke up, jumped out of bed, and exclaimed that you were awake, alive, and ready for the opportunities of the new day? Are you ready to face the day's challenges, excited to make an impact? On the other hand, do you meet the morning with a sense of drudgery and despair?

When was the last time you woke up early enough to watch the dawning of the new day? To see the rebirth of opportunity and possibility as the new day brings light to a darkened world.

When was the last time you stopped to drink deeply of the wonder of the morning and the gift of another day and just be amazed at life? The gift of a new day has arrived for you to proclaim, **"I am Awake, I am Alive, and I am ready to take on the World today!" When was the last time you shouted that you were Alive?**

I have had the great opportunity and privilege to see the new day arrive in 32 different countries, all 50 States, 500 miles from the North Pole, and deep in the South Pacific and it still amazes me. I still stand in awe as I watch the wispy tendrils of light pierce through the darkness and bring light and new life to the World.

Your journey through life and self-discovery is much like the start of a new day. As you grow, develop, and reinvent yourself, the tendrils of light tear through the darkness of your untapped potential and uncharted territories

The Greek Philosopher Socrates is quoted as saying, "The unexamined life is not worth leading." The most important investment you can make is in yourself. As you learn more, discover your life's purpose, and establish a vision for your future, the light shines through on your true self. That investment will determine your unstoppable life.

Each day you choose to operate in your unstoppable nature or we choose to operate out of your mediocre nature. The choice is made when you decide to proactively create your day or just live in the day and accept whatever comes your way. It is a choice of desire and fire or a choice of complacency and just good enough.

You are Unstoppable!

I am passionate about developing people and helping them reach their full potential by using a disciplined and deliberate approach. The beginning of an unstoppable life begins from the inside by taking charge of your life and by living on purpose.

In this book, you will hear three words that are the key to living an Unstoppable Life--**Responsibility, Accountability, and Hard Work!** Learn these three words and what they mean and you will live an Unstoppable Life!

In my first book, I stated that leadership principles are timeless, but unfortunately, we are not. We have an infinite ability to make an impact but we have a finite time here to make a difference and to leave some sort of legacy.

If you knew how much time you had to spend on earth, would you make different decisions about your life? Would you stop wasting time? Would you take yourself more serious? What will your legacy be?

You are Unstoppable! is about the intentional difference you make in your life by taking charge of your life and accepting who you are.

You are Unstoppable! is about you and the choices you make to become a better person. It is about you having the commitment, persistence, and perseverance to live your life and to be unstoppable when you face life's challenges.

You are Unstoppable! is about the effects and outcomes you want to create in your life. It is about taking responsibility for your growth and development and preparing yourself for the challenges of life. It is being serious with your approach to developing yourself to be ready for whatever life throws at you.

You are Unstoppable! is a Lifebook for your growth and development as a person and a leader. It is a slow cooking or crock-pot method of personal development versus a microwave method of personal development. You need to take the time to grow and develop yourself so when opportunities, crisis, and challenges come your way you are ready.

You are Unstoppable! is about you earning and maintaining your personal credibility and trustworthiness. Credibility and trustworthiness are the foundations of personal leadership. Credibility is the belief factor in your leadership. If you are credible and competent people will believe in you and follow your lead because they trust you.

In your professional, and in your private life, if people don't believe in you, they won't trust you. You begin building your credibility by exploring your inner core - your character, competence, courage, and commitment. You earn and maintain your credibility by clarifying your values, beliefs, and worldview. By understanding these three items you will understand how you make decisions and take action in your life.

You are Unstoppable! is about you and the choices you make to become a better person. It is about you having the commitment, persistence, and perseverance to live your life and to be unstoppable when you face life's challenges.

L.I.F.E. Books

I developed the L.I.F.E. book series to encapsulate my passion for developing people and helping them to live their lives to their utmost. The acronym L.I.F.E. stands for Leadership, Inspiration, Faith, and Empowerment. The philosophy behind L.I.F.E. books is detailed on the following pages:

Leadership

I am passionate about developing emerging, enduring, and experienced leaders and teaching them how to develop themselves using a disciplined and deliberate approach. All leadership begins from inside a person and must be developed and grown as they grow into emerging and enduring leaders.

Leadership starts with a condition of your heart – it is the desire and the passion to make a difference before it moves to your brain to implement an action plan to make a difference. Before you can make an impact on the world, you must first make an impact on yourself by discovering your purpose, your values, and by knowing who you are.

Inspiration

Inspiration is the ability to breathe life into your life and others. Inspiration is a positive influence and a positive reinforcement of life. It ignites desire, ignites creativity, and ignites innovation in inspired people. Your life's purpose is your daily inspiration for living abundantly. Your purpose excites you, energizes you, and fills you with a great sense of drive and determination.

Faith

Your faith provides you focus and vision for your life. It is your true north compass and GPS of self-awareness and self-management. Your faith is your lens to focus on how your talents, skills, gifts, and abilities will allow you to live on purpose. By focusing each day you can remove the noise and clutter of life to achieve your life's purpose. Living your faith daily matters immeasurably in everything you do. The better you pay attention to your life and faith, the greater your life outcomes. Your faith helps you to focus on your life choices, life opportunities, and life possibilities.

Empowerment

It is your life...OWN IT! Your life purpose empowers you and enables you to live life abundantly. Empowerment begins by taking responsibility for your life and being accountable for your actions. Empowerment is the courage to live passionately and purposefully each day. Anything is possible when you choose to believe in yourself, your life's purpose, and your talents, skills, and abilities. Your life purpose unleashes you to live your life and allows you to be unstoppable.

HOW TO USE THIS BOOK

Here is the bottom line: if you are looking for an easy fix to living an unstoppable life, then this book is not for you. The models, lessons, and concepts are tools – not a cure-all – for the hard work and discipline required to continuously grow, develop, and reinvent yourself.

If, however, you want to be a successful person in your profession and in life, then this book is a leadership and a life operator's manual to help you succeed. First, use the book as an informative guide of how to develop yourself and your leadership potential. Each of the Eight Disciplines of Personal Development discussed in this book are a piece of the overall F(X) and FORGE Models.

Second, use the book at the application level and use the models, leadership lessons, and exercises in your own life. Finally, read the book as a story of how you can make a difference in your life.

Now is the time to begin. True personal development is not something you do once in your life. It is a continuous process of growth, development, and reinvention. Your self-development journey never truly finishes. You are a masterpiece in progress.

You are Unstoppable! is your official invitation to continuously grow, develop, and reinvent your life and to leave a lasting legacy. If you are ready, turn the page and begin your adventure.

"I have for many years endeavored to make this vital truth clear; and still people marvel when I tell them that I am happy. They imagine that my limitations weigh heavily upon my spirit, and chain me to the rock of despair. Yet, it seems to me, happiness has very little to do with the senses. If we make up our minds that this is a drab and purposeless universe, it will be that, and nothing else. On the other hand, if we believe that the earth is ours, and that the sun and moon hang in the sky for our delight, there will be joy upon the hills and gladness in the fields because the Artist in our souls glorifies creation. Surely, it gives dignity to life to believe that we are born into this world for noble ends, and that we have a higher destiny than can be accomplished within the narrow limits of this physical life."

Helen Keller

CHAPTER 1

A CALL TO UNSTOPPABLE ACTION!

"Start by doing what's necessary; then do what's possible; and suddenly you are doing the impossible."
St. Francis of Assisi

Your Life is Unstoppable!

"All we have to decide is what to do with the time that is given us."
J. R. R. Tolkien

Visualize yourself getting ready for a race. This is the race of your life. Your heart is pumping and your chest is heaving with each breath. As you lower yourself in to the starting block, your legs start to shake with anticipation. Sweat drips from your forehead as you settle into the starting block.

You raise your head and begin to focus intently on the finish line. Your mind races as you wait for the starting gun to sound. You visualize each motion, each stride, and each step toward the finish line.

You are prepared.

You are ready.

You are focused.

The gun explodes and wakes you from your inner thoughts and you break out of the blocks. Your mind and body are flying down the track toward your goal. With each step, you are gaining speed and gaining ground toward the finish line.

You begin to run faster as you envision yourself crossing first. As you look toward the finish line, you notice that it seems farther away than before. You try to run faster, but your goal looks farther and farther away. Your breath is heavy now, your lungs are burning, and your legs feel like lead. You begin to slow your pace as your self-doubt creeps into your weary mind and you are afraid that you are incapable of finishing. As your pace slows down more and you finally begin to catch your breath, a runner comes alongside you and informs you that the race is not a sprint but a marathon.

Another wave of self-doubt and despair wash over you as you realize you are not prepared for a marathon. You are not ready for the long haul.

Your pace slows down to a crawl.

You begin to think about giving up.

You begin to lose faith in yourself.

You notice that the runner who came alongside has not left you. In fact, the runner has slowed down to your pace. The runner begins to encourage you with positive words that inspire you. With each new step, the runner encourages you to strive toward the finish line.

As hope builds inside you, you begin to feel the fire and passion you felt at the beginning of the race. Your steps become more steadfast and earnest. He encourages you to keep pressing toward the goal and not look back.

The runner has not left you and is pacing you step for step. As your pace quickens and your confidence builds, the runner says, **"Do you not know that in a race all the runners run, but only one gets the prize? Run in such a way as to get the prize."**

Your legs now are light and you feel that you will not grow weary, nor stop short of the end, or lose heart. Your eye is on the prize. You are now unleashed from everything that hinders you and you run with unwavering resolution.

You are unfettered.

You are determined.

You are driven.

You are an overcomer!

You now are standing at a fork in the road. Which road do you choose? Do you take the road that keeps you in your comfort zone and allows you to live unchallenged and safe? Or, do you choose the road that will challenge you, stretch you, grow you, and at times, consume you? The road you choose will dictate the life you will live.

Choose your road wisely…

> "Two roads diverged in a wood, and I-I took the one less traveled by, And that has made all the difference."
>
> **ROBERT FROST**

BE INSPIRED

To live an unstoppable life you need to live inspired and live for more than just yourself. When you live an unstoppable life you are an inspiration to others. On October 3, 1889, General Joshua L. Chamberlain said these inspiring words at the dedication of the Maine Monuments at Gettysburg Battlefield Cemetery:

> The inspiration of a noble cause involving human interests wide and far, enables men to do things they did not dream themselves capable of

before, and which they were not capable of alone. The consciousness of belonging, vitally, to something beyond individuality; of being part of a personality that reaches we know not where, in space and time, greatens the heart to the limits of the soul's ideal, and builds out the supreme of character. In great deeds, something abides.

On great fields something stays. Forms change and pass; bodies disappear; but spirits linger, to consecrate the ground for the vision-place of souls. And reverent men and women from afar, and generations that know us not and that we know not of, heart-drawn to see where and by whom great things were suffered and done for them, shall come to this deathless field, to ponder and dream; and lo! the shadow of a mighty presence shall wrap them in its bosom, and the power of the vision pass into their souls. This is the great reward of service, to live, far out and on, in the life of others.

Chamberlain was talking about the reward of service before self, in the ability to live your life – far beyond your own life – through service to others as an inspiration.

LIVE GREATLY

To live an unstoppable life you need to live greatly and not a life of mediocrity. Living greatly means you live a life that counts and live an abundant life. On April 23, 1910, President Teddy Roosevelt spoke these words at the Sorbonne in Paris, France:

> It is not the critic who counts; not the man who points out how the strong man stumbles, or where the

doer of deeds could have done them better. The credit belongs to the man who is actually in the arena, whose face is marred by dust and sweat and blood; who strives valiantly; who errs, who comes short again and again, because there is no effort without error and shortcoming; but who does actually strive to do the deeds; who knows great enthusiasms, the great devotions; who spends himself in a worthy cause; who at the best knows in the end the triumph of high achievement, and who at the worst, if he fails, at least fails while daring greatly, so that his place shall never be with those cold and timid souls who neither know victory nor defeat.

What he was talking about was living greatly and persevering throughout your life. Teddy Roosevelt was an example of an unstoppable life. When he was young, he suffered from asthma and other childhood sicknesses that could have left him weak and fragile throughout his early life. He challenged himself daily, developed his mind and body, and put himself in situations which required him to grow in order to overcome what life had put upon him. He challenged himself to live a life of greatness and abundance instead of a life of mediocrity.

CHANGE YOURSELF

To live an unstoppable life you need to change yourself every year and develop a life development plan. At the beginning of each new day, take the opportunity to start a portion of your life over by establishing new goals and new opportunities to change your life.

Change is not easy and takes some perseverance and will power. Anything is possible if you are determined to make it happen. All change begins with you and requires that you be committed to improving yourself. Dr. Viktor E. Frankl was an Austrian psychiatrist and neurologist who survived the Holocaust.

In October 1944, Frankl and his wife Tilly were sent to Auschwitz concentration camp for internment. Soon after arriving at Auschwitz, Viktor was sent to another concentration camp called Kaufering and his wife Tilly was sent to Bergen-Belsen. They would never see each other again and Tilly would die in the camp at the age of 24.

Viktor's mom would be murdered in the gas chambers in Auschwitz and his brother would die in the same camp. After being confined for three years and despite all the pain and suffering he endured, Dr. Viktor Frankl would write the book, *Man's Search for Meaning,* about his life in the concentration camp and his ability to decide how he would look at his circumstances. He chose his outlook in life.

In his book, two quotes stand out. "When we are no longer able to change a situation we are challenged to change ourselves" and "Everything can be taken from a man but one thing; the last of the human freedoms—to choose one's attitude in any given set of circumstances, to choose one's own way."

CHANGE YOUR MINDSET

Being unstoppable is a mindset. It is an unwavering belief in yourself, your abilities, and your capabilities. It is a belief in your unshakeable purpose and values. You have to believe in yourself with conviction and commitment. It is an awareness of your strengths and your challenges. It is about self-efficacy, self-awareness, and intentional clarity.

Once you have recognized your purpose and values and ingrained them, you begin to shape your unstoppable life. Unless you have an unwavering belief that you have something of value to offer this world you'll never be unstoppable.

The unstoppable mindset means that no matter what life tosses in your way, you can overcome it. It is about being fearless. Fear is a creation of your mind. It is a response to an uncertainty or an unknown. You need to be fearless in your life to be unstoppable. Being fearless is overcoming your feelings of fear and pushing through the uncertainty.

The only way to combat fear is to face your fear and take the necessary action to alleviate the fear. To get over fear, you have to take action. Being unstoppable is about making life choices. Life is a series of choices, and every choice you make defines you. The most important choice you can make is who you will become.

If you want to live an unstoppable life, you need to change your mindset and win the war of your thinking. You have tremendous inner strength as an individual and by applying this inner strength you can achieve what you want in life. By changing the way you think and applying different effects in your life, you can create new possibilities in your life.

TAKE CHARGE OF YOUR LIFE

The true key, if you want to live an unstoppable life, then you need to take 100% control of your life. Stop blaming others for your failures and faults and start accepting responsibility for your life.

If you want to succeed in life, then you need to create the outcomes of your life and quit letting others dictate your life. You are the owner of your success, failures, emotions, and feelings. So, take ownership of your life! To be truly unstoppable you must take charge of your life.

As long as you are bound to others for their acceptance and approval, you will not own your life. An unstoppable life is the freedom and liberty to express yourself authentically and unapologetically.

If you are consumed by the need for others to accept you, then you will be consumed trying to prove that you are worthy of their approval. You need to realize that you are worthy and loved in your own right without others justifying your existence. You need to have the courage to be yourself and accept who you are and what you have to offer the world.

It is your life…Own it! No one can change your life. You are the only you that can do it. It is up to you…you are the key to your life! If you want to realize victory in your life, then you have to take charge of your life. Along my journey through life, I have learned a few things for an unstoppable life.

- First, in order to be happy I must live my life according to my purpose and not what the World wants. I need to live authentically and congruent with purpose, values, and beliefs to live with integrity. This is important because my purpose drives me each day and gives me direction.

- Second, I actively decide not to sacrifice my values and beliefs on the altar of appeasement and enlightenment. My values and beliefs provide me the solid rock on which I stand. They are unwavering and ground me to reality.

- Third, I do not care what others think of my life, my values, beliefs, and my worldview. They are my anchor points in life. I am not trying to live their lives, I am living my own.

- Finally, I respect others for their values and beliefs and accept them for who they are. I am not talking about tolerance, but respect. I do not need to accept everything someone does with their life, but I do need to respect them and accept them for who they are. They are trying to live their life on this planet, too.

YOU ARE RESPONSIBLE

To begin taking ownership, you need to realize that each of us is given 24 hours each day to use as we wish-- 24 hours, no more no less; not a minute more. You can choose to use that time to create or change your life's outcomes or you can chose to waste the hours. The choice is yours.

How you choose to use the hours will determine if you will be successful or if you are wasting your time on earth. Each day, each hour, each minute is a gift of life and opportunity. You need to unwrap each day as a gift and see what you can do with the gift to make your life unstoppable! If you want to be successful, if you want to "be alive," if you want to have great passion for living on purpose, then you need to take responsibility for all aspects of your life—successes and failures. They are yours, you own them. Be intentional about your purpose in life.

Your thoughts, attitude, choices, and your decisions are the reason you are where you are today. Your life is the outcome of how you look at life, your attitude toward life, your choices, and decisions you make in life. You are the sum of these four. You are free to shape your attitude, free to change your thoughts, and free to make life choices and life decisions, but you must also understand the 2nd, 3rd, and 4th order of effects/consequences of these four areas.

YOU ARE ACCOUNTABLE

You are accountable for how you make your choices in life, how well you prepare yourself in life, how you persevere and persist against the odds, but moreover, you are accountable for your outlook or attitude about your life. You need to own your decisions, choices, and mistakes and be ready and willing to take the essential steps to learn from them. You must take accountability for your life or someone else will.

Where you are today in this moment of time is a direct result of your choices and decisions. But, where you go in the future depends on what you envision for your life and what actions you plan to take to make it happen.

You must quit blame shifting and start being accountable for your life. Stop making excuses for your decisions, they are under your control. Stop transferring blame to someone else or something for the outcomes of your decisions. When you blame others for your problems and challenges you deny personal responsibility and you give away your power of choice.

Life is not fair or equal. If it was fair and equal, we all would be living the same lifestyles. Life dealt your cards to you when you were born, now you must shape your life. Life will try to define you. It is your response to life though that will define you.

NEVER GIVE UP

To live an unstoppable life you must never give up on yourself, your dreams, and your life vision. You must never give up on believing in yourself, who you are, and what you are capable of doing. On October 29, 1941, Winston Churchill spoke these words at Harrow School after having survived the first major air war called the Battle of Britain:

> This is the lesson: never give in, never give in, never, never, never, never—in nothing, great or small, large or petty—never give in except to convictions of honour and good sense. Never yield to force; never yield to the apparently overwhelming might of the enemy…There was no flinching and no thought of giving in; and by what seemed almost a miracle to those outside these Islands, though we ourselves never doubted it, we now find ourselves in a position where I say that we can be sure that we have only to persevere to conquer.

He told the students at Harrow School to never give in and to never give up despite all odds being against them. Winston Churchill provided them a key to becoming unstoppable.

You must not give up on yourself, your dreams, or your desire to be unstoppable. You can choose to live a mediocre life or you can choose to push back on life and live a life of significance and impact. Seek to always be the very best person you can become each and every day.

The degree to which you can realize your dreams is contingent on you taking responsibility and never giving up on your life. No one can live your life or make your decisions. Living an unstoppable life is a choice and you must make the choice to be unstoppable.

MOMENT OF REFLECTION

After reading the above passages take a moment and ask yourself the following questions. Continue reading when you have answered them honestly

1. Are you living your Unstoppable life?
2. Are you living an Inspired Life?
3. Are you taking responsibility for your life?
4. Are you accountable for your life?

Taking Action!

In 1686, Sir Isaac Newton presented his three laws of motion in the *Principia Mathematica Philosophiae Naturalis*. Each law describes how motion is created and maintained. I use the three laws to indicate how you need to get yourself moving toward an unstoppable life.

Each time you are challenged you strengthen your commitment to overcoming life's challenges, you develop greater decision-making skills, and you reinforce your resiliency. Each time you are challenged you learn more about who you are and what you are capable of doing and becoming. Challenge yourself each day to stretch your life and clear a path for growth and development.

The First Law: Wake Up!

"Only those who will risk going too far can possibly find out how far one can go."
T. S. Eliot

Newton's First Law – An object at rest will stay at rest and an object in motion will continue to move at a constant speed in its original direction, unless acted upon by an external force. This law is often called "the law of inertia."

His first law states that every object remains at rest or in unchanging motion in a straight line unless compelled to change its state by the action of an external force. The object will not and cannot transform its state except when an external force is applied.

How does this apply to your life? You will continue to live in your comfort zones or inert spaces until some external or unbalanced force is employed that makes you want to grow and develop.

> Why is this important in your life? Your life will deteriorate and decay until you overcome inertia.

This external force could be a strong desire to grow your skills in order to be more competitive in the work place, it could be a robust goal for a better life, or it could be a mentor who is challenging you to reinvent yourself.

You need to take your life off cruise control and engage life. You need to take action to get out of your comfort zone or the good enough zone. Reflect on whether you are taking your talents, skills, and abilities for granted and are in danger of future failure due to complacency.

Get Out of Your Comfort Zone

Why do people have a hard time achieving an unstoppable life? They are afraid to get out of their comfort zone. What is a comfort zone? Your comfort zone can be your prison. I define a comfort zone as a zone of containment or as:

Captivity

Over

Me

From

Obtaining

Real

Triumphs

The number one thing I unfortunately see stopping people from continuously growing, developing, and reinventing themselves is their reluctance to step out of their comfort zone and take a risk.

They miss opportunity and success because they are afraid to take the risk. In order to grow and develop and to acquire additional knowledge, skill, and experience, you need to get out of your comfort zone.

Take the risk when an opportunity arises and step up to the challenge of expanding your horizons. Great opportunities in life are out there if you take the risk and seek them out. When you take the risk to step out and grow, it will stretch and grow you in all eight disciplines of personal development.

Significant opportunities of personal growth and success will arise throughout your lifetime. If you are ready to make positive changes and new breakthroughs in your life, you will need to embrace these opportunities and release yourself from your captivity.

One way to step out of your comfort zone is to face your fears and overcome them. How do you do that? You take small steps constantly out of your comfort zone and into the uncharted territory of your fears.

The largest fear you will need to tackle first is the fear of change. The fear of change is also the fear of growing, developing, and reinventing yourself.

The fear of growing, developing, and reinventing yourself is the fear that you will succeed and have to deal with all the changes of success. You do not need to fear the changes of success, you need to fear the regret of a life unchallenged and unfulfilled.

Your greatest power in life is the liberty to choose. It is the liberty to choose what you want to do with your life, where you want to go, and what you want to become.

No one can take this power away from you; it is yours alone. It is your choice to live unstoppable. Be bold in your life and declare yourself unstoppable.

Live Fearlessly!

The Second Law: Get Moving!

"Nothing in the world can take the place of Persistence. Talent will not; nothing is more common than unsuccessful men with talent. Genius will not; unrewarded genius is almost a proverb. Education will not; the world is full of educated derelicts. Persistence and determination alone are omnipotent. The slogan 'Press On!' has solved and always will solve the problems of the human race."
Calvin Coolidge

Newton's Second Law – When a force acts on an object, the object accelerates in the direction of the force. This means that objects with more mass requires more force to move the same distance as lighter objects.

How does this apply to your life? The longer you live in your comfort zone and allow yourself to stagnate, the more energy you will need to change your life. The energy required to change needs to be more than your desire to stay in your comfort zone. It will require hard work, persistence, and perseverance to move from the "as-is" to the "to-be."

The first step of action is the hardest and the most important. Expending energy to get your life moving is critically important to growing and developing. After you have started your growth and development, you will need to increase your enthusiasm and energy or momentum to keep yourself moving forward.

After your life is moving in the direction you want you need to keep the momentum by constantly seeking opportunities to grow and develop. There is no time to waste another moment of your lifetime in a state of flux.

Be the Change Agent of your Life

To live an Unstoppable Life you must be a change agent. You must confront complacency, mediocrity, uncertainty, and ambiguity in your life. Be proactive and begin to identify areas of opportunity in your life to change instead of waiting for them to present themselves at an inopportune time.

To live an Unstoppable Life you must have a change management strategy for your life. Your strategy means you are taking responsibility and accountability for your life and its outcomes. Your change management strategy empowers you to think critically about your life.

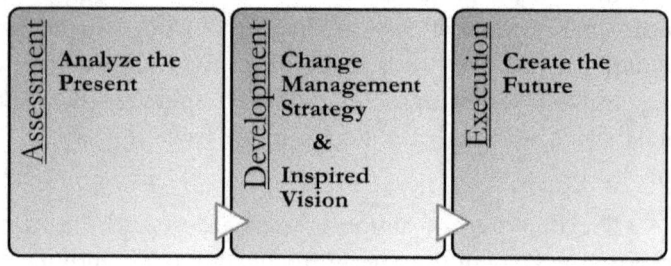

Your strategy allows you to analyze what you want to achieve, what new skills, aptitudes, and abilities you need, and when you need them in your life. Your growth and development are not a "one-time fill the square" event. They are constant and persistent. The principles of continuous growth, development, experience, and reinventing yourself are found in continuous change.

The Continuous Change process is a constant reminder that learning is a lifelong process and necessary to be a better leader every day. To keep pace with the ever-increasing demand of knowledge and pace of change in the world, you need to deliberately improve your personal and leadership ability.

Creating a life strategy or game plan will require you to reinvent yourself as you grow and develop. Reinventing yourself is the same process a Phoenix, the legendary bird that rises from the ashes to begin life anew, takes each time it goes through transformation.

To achieve something that you have never achieved before, you must reinvent yourself first. You must grow and develop qualities, skills, talents, and characteristics that you do not have today. You must learn to be flexible and adaptive to become that new person. To become truly successful in reinventing yourself, you need to clarify where you want to go, establish a plan, write it down, and believe it in your heart, mind, body, and soul.

Finally, why change? At the end of your life you should never look back in regret saying I should have, I wish I had, or maybe if…what you should say is, "Wow, what a ride…can I do it again?" Each of us is given only a finite amount of time; the choice is yours to waste it or make an impact with it.

Those who have felt the bitter taste of defeat understand and know what it takes to achieve victory and will continue to change and struggle until they have won. However, those who never try, who never get out of their comfort zone, or who just settle for second best will never live an amazing life. Now, go out and change your life!

Live Life Unlimited!

Third Law: No Pressure, No Diamonds

"No pressure, no diamonds."
Thomas Carlyle

Newton's Third Law – For every action there is an equal and opposite re-action. It means that for every force there is an equal but opposite reactionary force that is equal in size. What does this mean in your growth and development? It means, as you change and grow, the world will push back on you in the opposite direction equally hard as you press forward.

Life has a way of creating pressure on your life as you move forward. Persistence and perseverance are the sine qua non of Newton's third law. You need to keep pressing forward and pushing back on the world.

Persistence and perseverance are the abilities to maintain action despite the chaos. You press on even when you feel like quitting.

Thomas Carlyle, the Scottish philosopher and writer said, "No pressure, no diamonds." The name diamond is derived from the ancient Greek word Adámas or unconquerable. Diamonds are created by high temperatures and high pressure as it moves in the Earth.

Challenges Will Forge You

Success is to be measured not so much by the position that one has reached in life as by the obstacles which he has overcome while trying to succeed."
Booker T. Washington

In Chapter 1, I talked about the trials and tribulations Dr. Viktor Frankl went through during World War II and his response afterwards. His life was forged by those trials and tribulations, but he chose to shape his response to those challenges instead of allowing them to shape him.

In his book, *Man's Search for Meaning*, he states that in order to get through our trials and tribulations we must change our responses and ourselves. "We must never forget that we may also find meaning in life even when confronted with a hopeless situation, when facing a fate that cannot be changed."

Dr. Frankl's use of mental resilience, faith, and visualization techniques provided him the inner strength, persistence, and perseverance to create the outcomes he needed and wanted in his life.

> For what then matters is to bear witness to the uniquely human potential at its best, which is to transform a personal tragedy into a triumph, to turn one's predicament into a human achievement. When we are no longer able to change a situation--just think of an incurable disease such as inoperable cancer--we are challenged to change ourselves.

His self-awareness enabled him to choose how he would respond to the chaos that surrounded him. To be unstoppable you need to choose your responses and outcomes. Almost every minute of your life there is an opportunity to choose your response to life. Do you choose to proactively respond to life, negatively respond to life, or just react to whatever challenges life throws at you?

Your learning experiences arise from day-to-day activities, from moving out of your comfort zone and through your trials and challenges. Do not run from your problems or challenges, face them head on and tackle them. You need to tackle them as soon as they happen.

Why?

Because running from your problems will solve nothing. They will still be there after you stop running and they may actually grow larger. Is it easy to face your problems head on? No, but tackling them and solving them will build confidence and competence in your ability to make decisions and to cope with life's situations.

It isn't your problems that define you, but how you react to them and recover from them. Remember the whole purpose of being alive is to face challenges and setbacks, learn, adapt, and overcome them and turn them into your successes. Do not fall into the trap of following the path of least resistance. It may work for water, but it does not work in real life.

Life is not easy. It will try to define you especially when you plan to achieve success. Push back, forge ahead, and create greatness. It is through that forging process that your mettle is tested and you are forged into the person you want to become.

You need to maintain a positive perspective as you grow from your challenges. If you want to be unstoppable, you need to concentrate on the positives and look for the positive aspect in every situation. Your positive perspective will help you to create an unstoppable mindset.

To be truly successful you need to have a positive perspective in your life and about your life. If you allow yourself to turn to a negative perspective, you will never be able to reach an unstoppable mindset or successfully achieve your life goals.

Your challenges are stepping-stones of progress. You will learn more from your mistakes, errors, and challenges than you will learn from your successes. Why? Because it means you are taking the risk to live your life to its fullest. Do not be afraid of failing from time to time.

Take risks in your life. You will stumble and fail at times. In addition, when you do, get up, dust yourself off, and press forward with your life. A critical component of pressing forward is reviewing what your challenges have taught you.

Take the time to review your life lessons so you do not make the same choices again. After your review, press forward and continue to learn, grow, and develop. Everything that happens in your life is preparing and qualifying you for a moment that is yet to come.

Winston Churchill describes why it is vital we are prepared and qualified to lead our lives.

> To each there comes in their lifetime a special moment when they are figuratively tapped on the shoulder and offered the chance to do a very special thing, unique to them and fitted to their talents. What a tragedy if that moment finds them unprepared or

unqualified for that which could have been their finest hour.

Life will challenge, mold, and test you continuously throughout your existence. Remember, every challenge and test will teach you valuable life lessons that will grow, develop, and forge you. These are important life-shaping lessons.

Summary

Your unstoppable life is created by the same creative efforts of the world. You keep persisting and persevering toward an unstoppable life; the world will continue to press back and try to make you stop. Life will try to push you back into your comfort zone or inertia. You must continue to push back. If you want immense results, then be ready and energized to encounter immense challenges and pressures. Keep pressing back, keep pressing forward, and keep your eye on the prize. Be like the diamond and become unstoppable.

The beginning of an unstoppable life begins with the knowledge that is up to you to create and live your unstoppable life. No one else is responsible for your life or cares about your life as much you do. You must take responsibility for your life, believe in your possibilities, and look for your opportunities. You must change your mindset, see yourself, and live inspired each day. You have a choice today…Do you continue to live a life of mediocrity, or do you choose to live unstoppable?

Live Life Unleashed!

REFLECTION TIME

Give yourself some quiet time—20 minutes to start and reflect on who you truly are.

Personal Self-Assessment

Review the questions and select the answer that best fits how you assess your life at this moment.

I am in charge of my life.
    1 2 3 4 5 6 7 8 9 10

I take overwhelming action to change my life.
    1 2 3 4 5 6 7 8 9 10

I choose to live greatly.
    1 2 3 4 5 6 7 8 9 10

Life is what I make of it.
    1 2 3 4 5 6 7 8 9 10

I am awake and alive and ready for an Unstoppable Life.
    1 2 3 4 5 6 7 8 9 10

My choices determine my success.
    1 2 3 4 5 6 7 8 9 10

I have the ability to transform my life.
    1 2 3 4 5 6 7 8 9 10

I am responsible and accountable for my life.
    1 2 3 4 5 6 7 8 9 10

I never give up on myself.
    1 2 3 4 5 6 7 8 9 10

My life is full of possibilities.
    1 2 3 4 5 6 7 8 9 10

Self-Assessment Analysis

10-39 Points – You need to increase your self-awareness and self-efficacy. Take the time to do a deep dive on yourself to find out who you are and how to improve your life. If you want your life to be a masterpiece, you need to be the master of the pieces of your life.

40-70 Points – You have a good understanding of who you are but have areas that you need to grow and develop. Which area of your life do you need to improve? What effects do you need to implement to produce better outcomes?

71-89 Points – You are well on your way to being unstoppable in your life. You are living an abundant life and you understand the Principle of the Harvest. You know your true self and you are living your true purpose. Keep your eye on the prize and keep pressing forward.

90-100 Points – You are unstoppable. You are the Master of the Pieces of your life. However, do not stop now. You need to continue to grow, develop, and continually reinvent yourself.

UNSTOPPABLE TAKEAWAYS

Live Inspired

Each day is a choice of how you will live your day. You can choose to live inspired and grateful that you are alive. Or you can live uninspired and regret each day you walk the earth. Living inspired is looking at life as a positive experience full of opportunity and possibilities. It is living life to its fullest without regrets or I should haves.

Take Ownership

You are the architect of your life, so you need to take responsibility for your future and your outcomes. Take ownership of you choices and decisions. Taking ownership instead of assigning blame is a sign of inner strength and integrity. Understand that your life is not a mistake, it is a wonderful gift of life and opportunity. Own it!

ARE YOU BREATHING A.I.R?

Take a moment to reflect on your life. Look at the chart of actions, impacts, and results and use it as a road map to guide you on your Journey. What is your next step in your expedition?

ACTIONS	**IMPACT**
<ul><li>Be inspired</li><li>Never give up on yourself</li><li>Be accountable</li><li>Change your mindset</li></ul>	<ul><li>Live greatly</li><li>Grow and Develop</li><li>Positive life outlook</li></ul>
RESULTS	
<ul><li>Unstoppable Life!</li><li>Finish the Journey without regrets</li></ul>	

CHAPTER 2

IN THE BEGINNING....

"Start by doing what's necessary; then do what's possible; and suddenly you are doing the impossible."
St. Francis of Assisi

It all Begins with a Choice

"And there were always choices to make. Every day, every hour, offered the opportunity to make a decision, a decision which determined whether you would or would not submit to those powers which threatened to rob you of your very self, your inner freedom; which determined whether or not you would become the plaything of circumstance, renouncing freedom and dignity to become molded into the form of the typical inmate."
Viktor Frankl

A great part of my job during my time in the military was the one-on-one counseling meetings with young enlisted personnel called first-term Airmen. As an opening to our counseling session, I traditionally asked them, "Why are you here?" For the most part the Airmen had a clear answer for joining the Air Force.

"I joined for the education."

"I joined because my father/mother was in the Air Force."

"I joined to see the world."

"I joined to serve my Country."

"I joined to do something with my life."

The next five questions after I understood **WHY** they joined the Air Force stumped many of the Airmen. The five questions after the why were:

- Who are you?
- What do you want to become?
- Where do you want to end up in life?
- How do you plan to achieve your end state?

- When do you plan to start changing your life?

Ninety percent of their answers were vague or ambiguous and lacked the concreteness of purpose to achieve what they envisioned for their life.

The Airmen answered the why question with confidence and clarity because they knew why they were there. Unfortunately, most of the Airmen struggled with the other questions because they did not take the time to think and plan their future past the present.

As the conversation continued, I informed them:

> You need to forge ahead or you will fall behind in life and in the Air Force. I need you to be engaged every day in developing your skills, talents, and capabilities to help us to achieve our mission in the Air Force. However, you need to be engaged with your life every day so you can achieve your purpose, vision, and goals in life.

At the end of the counseling session, each Airman had a homework assignment due to me in a month—to answer the five questions completely and bring the answers back to me.

Through this technique, I helped several Airman design a life action plan with goals and outcomes. This process eventually became what I call the FORGE Discovery Process.

The FORGE Discovery Process

Everything starts with you. You are the one that brings your dreams to creation. You are the founder of the past, present, and future you. You possess the unstoppable power to create a positive and amazing life. There is virtually no limit of who you can become and what you can do with an unstoppable belief in yourself.

FORGE DISCOVERY PROCESS

WHY DO YOU WANT AN UNSTOPPABLE LIFE? Why is it important to live an unstoppable life? What do you plan to do with an unstoppable life?

WHO ARE YOU? A self-discovery of who you are through your purpose, values, beliefs, worldview, and your character.

WHAT DO YOU WANT TO BECOME? What does your future look like? What is your vision and mission for your life?

WHERE DO YOU WANT TO END UP IN LIFE? What do you want out of life? What kind of job, lifestyle, and achievements do you want?

HOW DO YOU PLAN TO ACHIEVE YOUR END STATE? What is your action plan to achieve your unstoppable life? What is your timeline and milestones for achieving your unstoppable life?

WHEN DO YOU PLAN TO START CHANGING YOUR LIFE? What actions can you take today to start living an unstoppable life?

The FORGE Discovery Process is about the choices you need to make in your life. It is about being proactive, taking charge, and leading your life. With an unstoppable belief in yourself and your abilities, you can dream bigger dreams, set greater goals and action plans, and commit yourself to achieving your vision and purpose in life.

The truth is that, if you develop an unstoppable life, your whole world will be different. Your life gets better when you change your life to live an unstoppable life.

The FORGE Discovery Process allows you to define the outcomes that you choose to bring to reality in your life. The FORGE Discovery Process is about making the choices each day to determine your destiny and future life. Your Unstoppable life is a result of the decisions your make, the actions you take, and challenges and trials that you overcome.

The process begins with six defining questions that you need to answer before you can start authoring your unstoppable life. By answering these six questions, you can make a positive and amazing difference in your life.

The FORGE Discovery Process guides you to start authoring your unstoppable life and achieving your life's goals. It also helps you define your purpose, your vision, and your life.

When you understand your past and your present life then you can define the outcomes of your future. Without a clear understanding of your life, you will continue to remain in the same state of being as you are today.

Without changing the outcomes of your life, you will continue to get the same results and never achieve your unstoppable life. When you change your outcomes, you will change your circumstances in life.

Your Choices Determine Your Destiny

Your choices each day determine what outcomes happen in your life. It is by choice, not by chance, that will determine your life. An Unstoppable Life begins by taking responsibility for your choices.

You make choices in your life each day. You can choose to be proactive and take control of your decisions or you can react to them like a victim of circumstance. Your decisions are the single most important factor that drives your unstoppable life.

Your decisions are the A.I.R. (Action, Impact, and Result) or the breath of life you take each day to live. Each decision is made from your action, the impact of the action, and the results of that action.

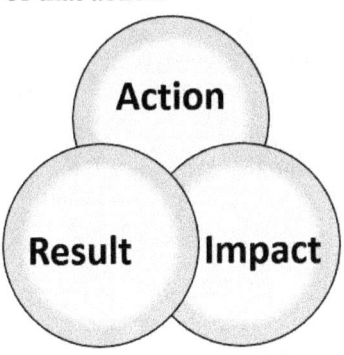

You are responsible and accountable for your decisions. No one is responsible for the consequences of that decision, only you. Each time you make a decision you need to make sure the outcome and result is what you want.

If your daily decisions are in alignment with your values, beliefs, and worldview, then you are moving forward in your dreams, aspirations, and goals achievement.

You are unstoppable and you have unleashed your inspired life. Your choices determine who and what you are and can become. C.S Lewis, English professor and author of *The Chronicles of Narnia*, stated,

> Every time you make a choice, you are turning the central part you – the part that chooses – into something a little different than what it was before. Taking your life as a whole, with innumerable choices, you are slowly turning this thing into a heavenly creature or a hellish creature.

Life is about the decisions and actions you

make each day.

All of us are living with the decisions we made yesterday, last year, and years gone by. The choices we made determined who we are, what we are, and where we are today. All decisions have consequence

The Actions you take in life Impacts the way you achieve your Results

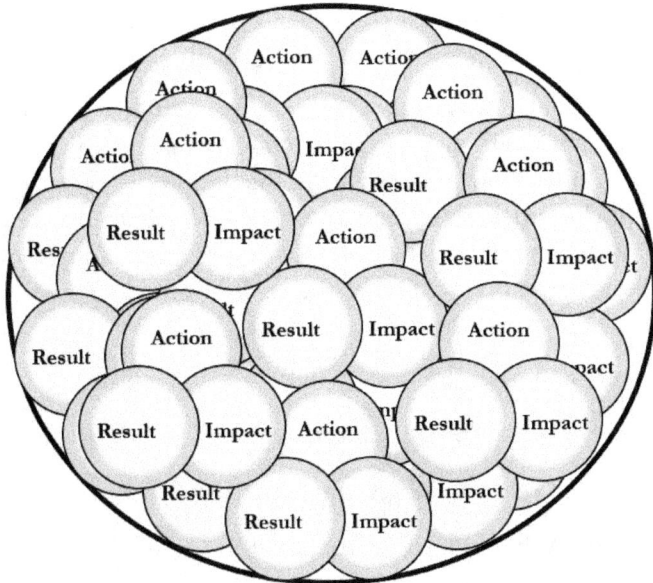

Many of us made choices without a clear understanding of the kinetic impact the 2nd, 3rd, or 4th order of effects of that decision would have on our futures.

> To be an effective decision-maker you must be proactive and stay abreast of issues and opportunities in your life.

You need to identify and evaluate the information and then use the information to make a decision, take action, and critically analyze the outcome to understand the 2nd, 3rd, or 4th order of effects of the decision.

You need to take the time when you make life decisions to reduce ambiguity and uncertainty, solved, and unresolved issues and problems, and to take advantage of life's opportunities. As soon as you recognize critical issues and problems, you need to take action to resolve them. The quicker you take action to resolve those issues and problems, the sooner you remove potential roadblocks and obstacles that may impede your growth and development.

When you take the time to become fully aware of new life opportunities, you can then create new possibilities for yourself. After you identify the issues, problems, and opportunities, you need to determine what you want as your desired outcomes. Defining your decision is contingent on identifying the desired outcomes you want to achieve and the decision criteria.

You need to decide the "What:"

- What do you want to achieve?
- What results are you expecting?
- What impact do you want to make?
- What do you hope to accomplish?

Kinetic Effects

Picture yourself standing beside a lake and you throw a small stone into the lake. First thing you will notice will be the impact of the stone on the lake's surface.

- The first order of effect will be the splash the stone creates.
- The second order of effect is the ripples the splash creates.
- The third order of effect is the stone landing on the bottom of the lake.

- The fourth order of effect is the reverse ripples created as the second order ripples hit the shoreline.

- An indirect effect occurs when your decision creates a direct effect that produces additional ripple effects. An indirect effect of your decision to throw the rock is a flock of birds fly out of the trees after hearing the splash of the rock.

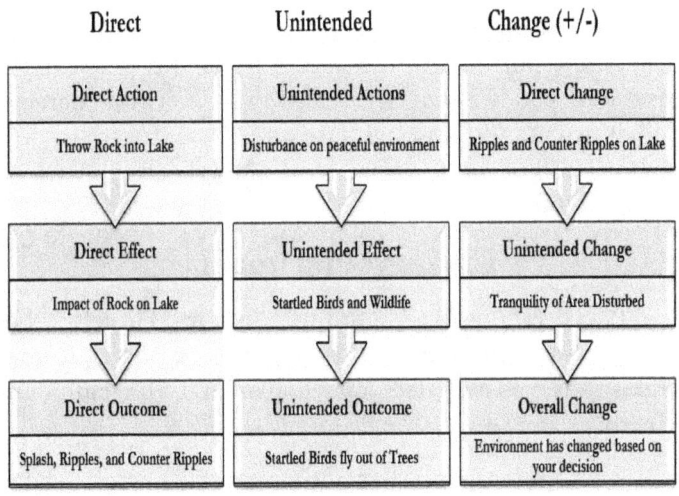

If you make life decisions unconsciously or without the thought of the kinetic effects, you can do more damage in your life versus good. However, if you make life decisions intentionally, you can transform the course of your life.

Your decisions will have both direct and indirect effects and 2nd, 3rd, or 4th order of effects. When making your decision you need to understand the 2nd, 3rd, or 4th order of effects that your decision will have on your life.

Each of your decisions has that kinetic effect on your life, the people around you, and your desired outcome. When you understand the "what you want to accomplish" and the direct and indirect effects of that decision, you can create the "how you want to accomplish it" decision.

Each time you make decision that are congruent and consistent with your values, beliefs, and purpose you strengthen your character authenticity and personal integrity.

Conversely, each time you compromise your values, beliefs, and purpose for the sake of popularity peers, or the easy way you weaken and chip away at your character authenticity and personal integrity. You begin to lose yourself and begin down the road of mediocrity.

Create your Timeline

Nosce Te Ipsum is Latin for "Know Thyself." The saying is attributed to many Greek and Roman philosophers to include Socrates, Aristotle, Heraclitus, and Cicero.

This theme of understanding yourself is also a key principle many of today's leadership authors point to as the beginning point for all leaders. Knowing yourself improves your capability to be flexible and adaptive in different situations, allowing you to work diplomatically and skillfully with others during challenging and demanding problems.

It allows you to use the right capabilities at the right time and in the right situational context. Knowing yourself likewise provides you more confidence in developing yourself for the future.

Part of knowing yourself is the creation of your life timeline. Why create a timeline? A life timeline is a personal review of your life from birth to the present time. It is an autobiography of your life. It is how you begin to tell your message to the world. It is your life story.

The benefit of creating your life timeline is that it provides you vital information of your life and what shaped you. As you write out your timeline, you will begin to see themes and patterns of your life.

Your timeline will point out patterns of growth and development, outcomes of your decisions, your responses to challenging events, and it will provide personal insight into your life's purpose.

Your timeline is a deep dive on the major events in your life, major life achievements, major life decisions, life-changing moments, life-affirming moments, setbacks, failures, and significant events that changed your life.

Finally, your timeline will provide you with an opportunity to shape and mold your future by allowing you to make better decisions and by allowing you to put life-changing effects into your life. Remember, to live an unstoppable life, you need to know yourself.

Summary

The beginning of an unstoppable life begins with the knowledge that is up to you to create and live your unstoppable life. No one else is responsible for your life or cares about your life as much you do.

You must take responsibility for your life, believe in your possibilities, and look for your opportunities. You must change your mindset, see yourself, and live inspired each day.

When you do not take responsibility to develop and manage your life – someone else will. When you fail to take responsibility for your life, you become susceptible to what others expect from you and your life.

When you do not take responsibility to create your life outcomes then you give away your Unstoppable power to others to create your life outcomes. Through their influence and power over your life, they will mold and shape your destiny. You have a choice today…Do you continue to live a life of mediocrity, or do you choose to live unstoppable? Choose to believe in yourself

- Choose to live on purpose
- Choose to live your values
- Choose to live your faith
- Choose to live with courage and confidence
- Choose to live with integrity
- Choose to create your outcomes

Live Life Courageously!

REFLECTION TIME

Give yourself some quiet time—20 minutes to start and reflect on who you truly are.

Personal Self-Assessment

Review the questions and select the answer that best fits how you assess your life at this moment.

I am forging ahead in my life.

    1 2 3 4 5 6 7 8 9 10

I choose to keep moving forward in life.

    1 2 3 4 5 6 7 8 9 10

I will not fall behind.

    1 2 3 4 5 6 7 8 9 10

My life is built around my choices and decisions.

    1 2 3 4 5 6 7 8 9 10

I understand the kinetic effect of my decisions.

    1 2 3 4 5 6 7 8 9 10

My decisions breath A.I.R.

    1 2 3 4 5 6 7 8 9 10

I can change my outcomes with better decisions.

    1 2 3 4 5 6 7 8 9 10

My life is my message to the world.

    1 2 3 4 5 6 7 8 9 10

I am writing a novel of inspiration with my life.

    1 2 3 4 5 6 7 8 9 10

My life is a product of my positive outlook on life.

    1 2 3 4 5 6 7 8 9 10

Self-Assessment Analysis

10-39 Points – You need to increase your self-awareness and self-efficacy. Take the time to do a deep dive on yourself to find out who you are and how to improve your life. If you want your life to be a masterpiece, you need to be the master of the pieces of your life.

40-70 Points – You have a good understanding of who you are but have areas that you need to grow and develop. Which area of your life do you need to improve? What effects do you need to implement to produce better outcomes?

71-89 Points – You are well on your way to being unstoppable in your life. You are living an abundant life and you understand the Principle of the Harvest. You know your true self and you are living your true purpose. Keep your eye on the prize and keep pressing forward.

90-100 Points – You are unstoppable. You are the Master of the Pieces of your life. However, do not stop now. You need to continue to grow, develop, and continually reinvent yourself.

UNSTOPPABLE TAKEAWAY

Discover Who You Are

The first step to living an unstoppable life is to discover who you are and what you want out of life. The FORGE Discovery Process helps you to start the process of self-discovery. It is the first stepping-stone to your unstoppable life.

ARE YOU BREATHING A.I.R?

Take a moment to reflect on your life. Look at the chart of actions, impacts, and results and use it as a road map to guide you on your Journey. What is your next step in your expedition?

ACTIONS	**IMPACT**
• Decision-making • Discover who you are • Create your Timeline	• Increased self-awareness and insight

RESULTS
• Better decisions and create a great life message

CHAPTER 3

SELF-LEADERSHIP IS THE KEY

"The dogmas of the quiet past are inadequate to the stormy present. The occasion is piled high with difficulty, and we must rise with the occasion. As our case is new, so we must think anew and act anew. We must disenthrall ourselves, and then we shall save our country."
Abraham Lincoln

"*Knowing others is intelligence; knowing yourself is true wisdom.*"
Tao Te Ching

A Great Way of Life!

"Twenty years from now you will be more disappointed by the things that you didn't do than by the ones you did do. So throw off the bowlines. Sail away from the safe harbor. Catch the trade winds in your sails. Explore. Dream. Discover."
Mark Twain

In 1982, I made a decision to join the United States Air Force. It was a life changing decision. In August 1983, I arrived at Lackland Air Force Base, in San Antonio, Texas to start my introduction to the Air Force in Basic Military Training (BMT). It was the start of an inspiring journey that would last 28 years and take me to 32 different countries and all 50 States.

Upon arrival to BMT, I realized a few things right of way. First, Texas is hot and muggy in August and you break a sweat just by breathing air.

Second, I had no control of my life for the next eight weeks. I was now the official property of the United States Air Force. However, it was the life lessons that I learned at BMT change my outlook on life. There are seven life lessons that I took away from BMT that I started me on my journey.

1) **Self-Discipline** – If you want to succeed in BMT you need self-discipline. Upon arrival to Lackland Air Force Base, you learn the meaning of discipline. You learn to fold you clothes, you learn how to march, you learn how report to your leaders, and you learn how to make your bed in accordance with the standards. It teaches you to have discipline and ultimately self-discipline.

Lesson learned: To be successful in life you need self-discipline, self-control, and self-motivation. You need to train and develop yourself to prepare for the uncertainty of life's challenges. Furthermore, you need to be a self-starter and be able to create and maintain your own motivation. You need a discipline approach to living your life.

2) **Hard Work** – BMT teaches you that hard work is a part of day-to-day life. So get used to it. Nothing is free or easy in the military. If it is important to you and you want to achieve it you need to work hard for it.

    Lesson learned: Hard work is the price you pay to achieve great things in your life. Let me reemphasize this point. There are no free rides everything has a cost. Hard work achieves great things in life. Free rides achieve mediocrity. You have to pay the price to be Unstoppable.

3) **Decisions** – My Training Instructor (TI) informed us on the third day of BMT that "You will make or break your military career on the quality of your decisions. Everything you do from this day forward is a result of the decisions you make." His words ring true today.

    Lesson Learned: All life is a decision. No matter what you do, you are making choices and decisions. Some decisions will work the way you planned and some will not. Nevertheless, you own the decision and its outcome. So take the time to think about the outcome before you make the decision.

4) **Planning and Preparation** – During BMT each day is planned and organized to maximize your day.

There is no wasted time in BMT. Each day builds on the next and moves you closer to the goal of graduating and moving on to your technical school. This disciplined approach prepares you for a career in the military.

Lesson Learned: If you want to move ahead in the life you must learn how to plan and prepare to maximize your time to achieve your life goals. Time is short so use it wisely.

5) **Responsibility and Accountability** – Along with my TI's information on decisions he constantly drilled into us that we are responsible and accountable for our actions in the Air Force. He did not want to hear our excuses or hear us pass the blame on circumstances or on another person. You are responsible and accountable for how your Air Force career turned out. **NO ONE ELSE.**

Lesson learned: You are responsible and accountable for your life and its eventual outcome. No one else is responsible or accountable for how your life turns out. Your life is the product of your decisions, how well you planned your life, and your actions.

6) **Actions** – Each order given during BMT required some type of action in order to carry out the order. Marching is a good example of action applied to a command or order. When the TI yelled "Forward, March", you put your feet and brain into action to carry out the command. You move forward. When the TI said "Right, Face" you turned right.

Lesson Learned: Your decisions require actions to make them a reality. A decision to do something without an action applied is just a passing thought and useless. Your actions to your decisions will determine what you can and will achieve. You must take action in life to achieve success.

7) **Persistence and Perseverance** – The best BMT lesson I learned was to never give up on yourself or your goals. BMT is intended to break you down then build you up so you are ready for the challenges of the military. BMT teaches you to persevere and reach for your goals.

Lesson Learned: I will be the first to tell you that the military life is not easy nor is it for everyone. It takes time to learn how to adapt and adopt your life to military standards. However, you learn very quickly what you are made of and what you are capable of doing. It teaches you to persist and persevere if you want to have successful career.

Basic Military Training provided a foundation for growth and development through a disciplined and focused approach to life. It taught me that whatever you want or need in life take time, action, and hard work to achieve. These lessons have been invaluable to me throughout my career and in life. These valuable life lessons helped me shape and mold my Air Force Career and life through a disciplined approach to life.

A Disciplined Approach

I served 28 years in the United States Air Force, learned quite a bit about the reason, and need for discipline. Discipline for many people is a negative word meaning restriction and no freedom. To me, discipline means freedom and opportunity by taking charge of my life and creating the outcomes I want in life.

Through an intentional an disciplined approach, I prepared myself for opportunities that I would not have if I lived life in a laissez faire manner. Through a disciplined approach, I learned to accept responsibility and accountability for my decisions and actions, which allowed me the freedom to accept my failures and successes equally.

In my first book, *F(X) Leadership Unleashed*, I introduced the F(X) Leadership Development Process. The process represents what I learned over the past 30 years of serving as a supervisor and frontline leader in the military and serving in leadership roles in several non-profit organizations.

It was a way of thinking about my development as a leader, personally and professionally, and the effect of it on my life. There are three main models associated with the F(X) Leadership Development Process:

- The F(X) Model – The F(X) Model is a symbolic way of thinking about the inside-out process of developing your leadership skills and life skills first before investing and developing others. All leadership begins from inside you.

- The Inspire or Retire Theorem – A mathematical mnemonic of your leadership responsibility to the people in your organization. It is a way to remember to always Inspire or Retire!

- The Leadership Based Outcomes/Mindset Model – The LBO/M five-stage cycle process is from the briefing titled, *Effects-based Operations: Change in the Nature of War*, authored by Lieutenant General

David A. Deptula (Retired), and first published by the Aerospace Education Foundation in 2001.

The F(X) Leadership Development Process is a deliberate and disciplined approach to developing and growing yourself. Why is a disciplined approach important in personal development?

How you got to where you are in life at this moment in time is based on the sum total of the decisions you have previously made in your life. The clearer your life's picture, the more likely you will achieve it. A disciplined approach to personal development ensures that you are prepared to lead yourself in order to lead others.

Developing a disciplined plan outlines your self-improvement goals, strategies, and outcomes that will help you take advantage of opportunities and be prepared to meet challenges. A disciplined approach allows you to prioritize and categorize goals so you can target which goals will provide the most benefit first.

You are the key to the F(X) model and to your success. The function of (x) is you.

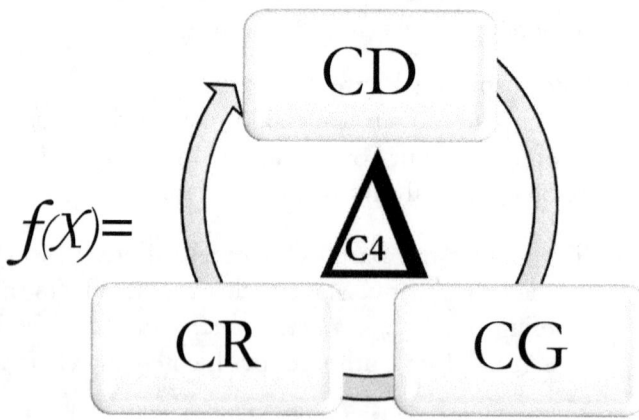

You are Unstoppable!

Δ

- The Greek symbol DELTA represents change or difference. Change as a leader is a constant. The changes you make daily and throughout your life will make a difference in your leadership and your life.

C4

- Character, Competence, Courage, and Commitment – C4 is the most explosive part of the function of (x) because it represents who you are deep down inside, your abilities, your strengths, and your passion.

CD

- Continuous Development – As a leader you must continually develop yourself professionally, technically, mentally, spiritually, and physically to stay on the leading edge and to be the example for others to follow.

CG

- Continuous Growth – Growth is the discipline and commitment to apply and incorporate the learned development to your character and leadership abilities.

CR

- Continuously Reinventing Yourself – As you grow and develop your character, your leadership abilities, your competence, and your capabilities, you will continually reinvent who you are and what you are capable of accomplishing.

THOMAS S. NAROFSKY

The Unstoppable Model

"We all have dreams. But in order to make dreams come into reality, it takes an awful lot of determination, dedication, self-discipline, and effort."
Jesse Owens

The Unstoppable Model builds upon the original F(X) Leadership Development Model but solely focuses on personal development instead of organizational development. The two main parts of model are the inner core and the outer rings. The inner core consists of the Delta symbol and the C4 and your values, beliefs and worldview. The outer rings contain the discovery processes of your Personal Insight and personal Mastery.

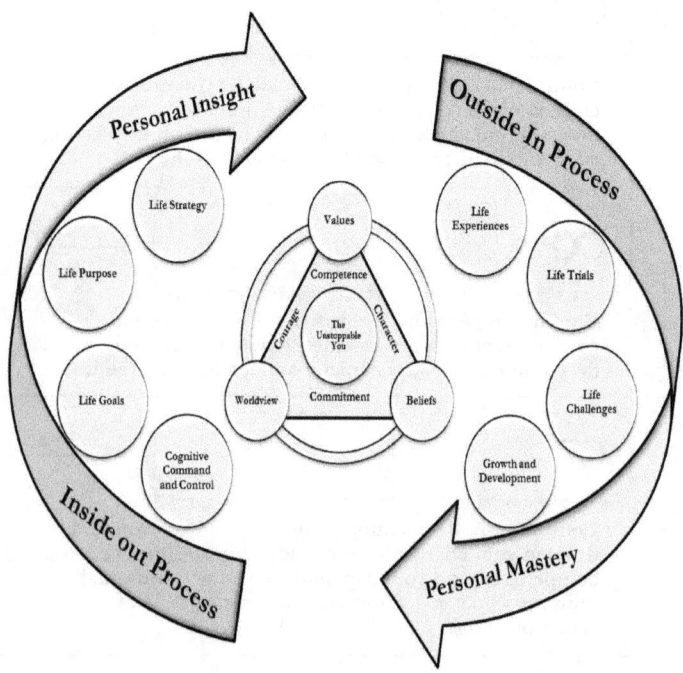

The Unstoppable model focuses on a whole person concept and is a disciplined inside-outside approach to growth, development, and reinvention focused on all aspects of your life.

The Unstoppable Model is a constant look at your life as you grow, develop, and learn more about who you are and what you are capable of throughout your life.

> Each day is a choice to live an Unstoppable and Inspired life through your ability to lead yourself each day. The foundation of your success begins with personal leadership and your personal commitment to be accountable and responsible for your life.

You must lead yourself and take ownership of your life. Personal leadership is a key part of living an Unstoppable Life and living abundantly.

The Unstoppable Model is a holistic inside-out process that begins with you developing the inner core of your life before you move to the outside areas. It is recognition that you must constantly grow, develop, and reinvent yourself in order to be unstoppable and to be the very best you can be every day.

As a life leader, you must learn to lead yourself effectively each day and stay focused on achieving your life goals.

The Inner Core

The first part of the Unstoppable Model is C4—Character, Competence, Courage, and Commitment and the Delta Symbol. As discussed previously this is the most explosive part of your life and is constantly changing and developing each day.

Your values, beliefs, and worldview are the next part of the model and are the constants in your life. Your core values drive your life decisions and your decisions about when you want to lead, how you want to lead, and how much you want to lead

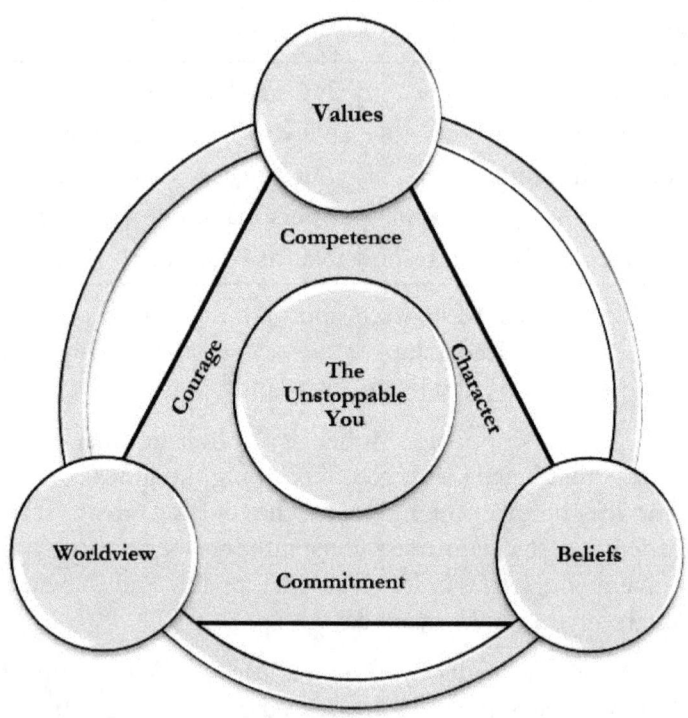

These two parts make up the inner core of the Unstoppable Model. Your character, competence, courage, commitment, values, beliefs, and worldview are key parts of being Unstoppable. These provide you with the solid foundation you need to build upon each day to create an Unstoppable Life. By understanding your inner core you create greater life opportunities through your outer rings.

The Outer Rings

The outside parts of the Unstoppable Model represent two areas of personal growth and development—Personal Insight and Personal Mastery. Developing Personal Insight and Personal Mastery is an important and intentional self-investment in our lives.

It is a deliberate lifelong development and growth process in order to know ourselves better each day. Through this process, we can master our strengths to increase our credibility and to leverage them to create an inspiring future.

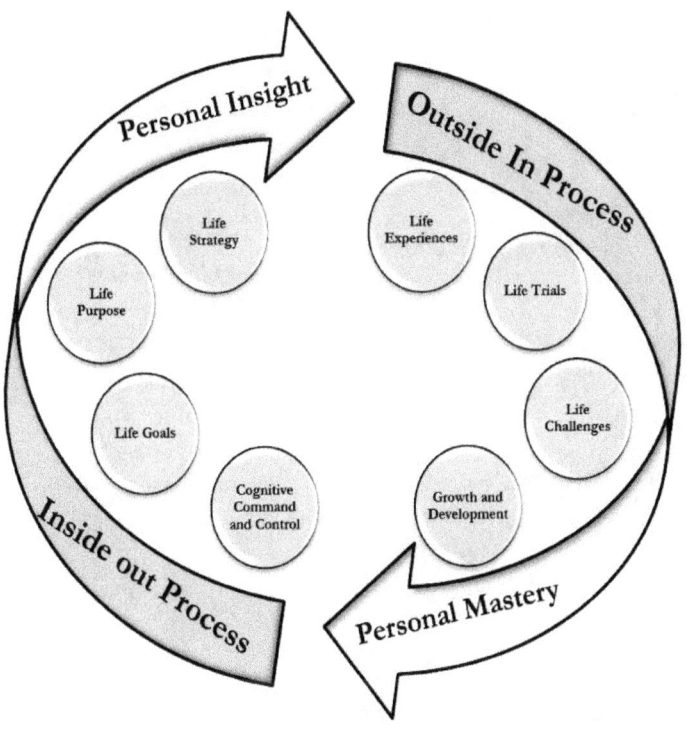

Personal Insight

Personal Insight is an intentional process of discovering and understanding who you are, what you believe in, and your life purpose. Personal Insight embraces the concept of "Nosce Te Ipsum"--Know yourself. It is an inward look at your life through a deliberate process of reflection and self-study. It is an honest self-assessment about our strengths and weaknesses.

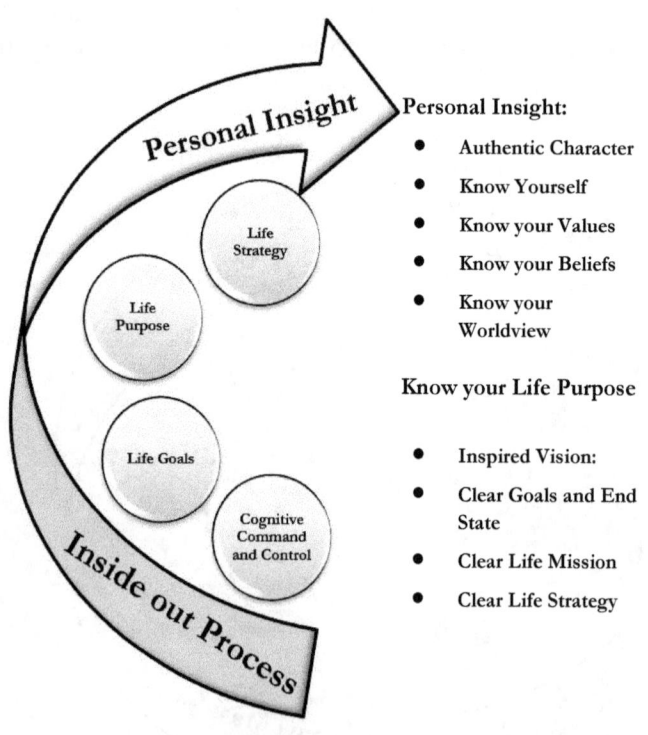

Personal Insight:
- Authentic Character
- Know Yourself
- Know your Values
- Know your Beliefs
- Know your Worldview

Know your Life Purpose

- Inspired Vision:
- Clear Goals and End State
- Clear Life Mission
- Clear Life Strategy

Personal Insight helps you to know your values, beliefs, worldview, life purpose, and define your Authentic

Character. Personal Insight provides you with the personal confidence you need to plan and prepare for the future through an increased self-awareness of what you want to achieve in life. This self-awareness provides you increased and strategic clarity to develop an inspiring life vision .

Using self-insight, you can determine the approach you need to take to become more effective and proactive in your life. It allows you to meet the challenges of life head on without fear or uncertainty. Truly understanding who you are and how you operate as a person you can better understand how to grow, develop, and reinvent yourself for life.

Through Personal Insight, you establish an inspiring vision for your life; define a Mission Statement, Life Goals, and a Life Strategy to achieve an Unstoppable Life.

Personal Insight utilizes the C4 Model, the FORGE Discovery Process, the Unstoppable Matrix, planning preparation, and passion from the 6P Focus model.

Personal Mastery

Personal Mastery is a commitment to self-discipline, continuous growth, and development. It is a disciplined approach to honing your personal competence by developing you eight personal development areas—personal, professional, leadership, spiritual, emotional, physical, mental, and social disciplines.

Personal Mastery is about being intentionally prepared for life's challenges and day-to-day life. Self-efficacy is important part of self-mastery. Self-efficacy is honing your skills, talents, capabilities, abilities, and gifts in a disciplined manner to increase your life effectiveness. Through a disciplined approach to growth and development, you build your self-mastery to ensure you have the talents and skills to match your increased self-awareness of your Personal Insight.

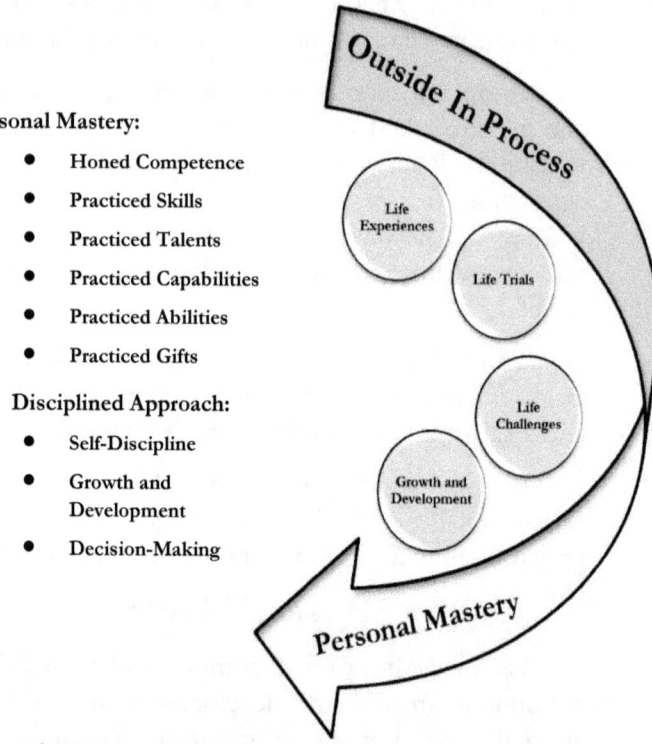

Personal Mastery:
- Honed Competence
- Practiced Skills
- Practiced Talents
- Practiced Capabilities
- Practiced Abilities
- Practiced Gifts

Disciplined Approach:
- Self-Discipline
- Growth and Development
- Decision-Making

Through Personal Mastery, we are stretched, refined, and forged by life's challenges and helps us to thrive in a volatile, uncertain, complex, and ambiguous world.

Personal mastery is a commitment to becoming the master of your of your life skills, talents, gifts, abilities, and capabilities.

It is a commitment to continuous discipline, hard work, and paying the price to developing, growing, and reinventing your life potential. Personal Mastery is a key component of your life and utilizes the F(X) Deliberate Learning, the F(X) FORGE Model, and performance, persistence, and perseverance from the 6P Focus Model.

Eight Disciplines of Personal Development

There are eight disciplines of personal development in the Unstoppable Model. These areas of development help you grow and develop holistically and congruently. The eight areas are developed and grown through personal insight and personal mastery.

Personal

The Personal Discipline is the C4 of your life. This area has been developing since you were born and never truly stops growing and developing. However, it can become stagnate if you stay in your comfort zone. This discipline is the most important to develop and grow because it is the foundation of your professional and leadership discipline areas.

The Personal Discipline is You the Person. This discipline is focused on who you are—your purpose, values, character, and worldview. This discipline is also focused on how you communicate, show respect, extend dignity; build relationships, live with integrity and trust, and how resilient you are in your life.

Professional

The Professional Discipline is about your career and professional life. It does not define you as a person but it is the area of your learned expertise. It is a vital part of your life as it helps you meet areas in Maslow's Hierarchy of

Needs Model. The Professional Discipline is concerned with you, your career, and the skills needed to succeed. This discipline focuses on your experience, technical skills, management skills, talents, and aptitudes. This discipline also focuses on the necessary education, training, and development you need to keep you competent in your expertise.

Leadership

The Leadership Discipline is about you as a leader and your leadership ability and capability. You must continue to develop this area of expertise as you grow your professional expertise. This discipline is concerned with both your self-leadership and your team and organizational leadership. This discipline focuses on your leadership skills, attitude, aptitude, leadership experience, and overall development. This discipline also focuses on your leadership opportunities, building alliances and partnerships, leadership authenticity, selfless service attitude, talent development, and culture creation.

Spiritual

The Spiritual Discipline is about you as a spiritual person. This discipline is concerned with your faith, resiliency and your ability to believe in a higher purpose. This discipline focuses on you seeking and finding personal meaning and purpose for your life through soul-searching, prayer, and mediation. This discipline also focuses on strengthening your beliefs, principles, and values to sustain you as a person through self-awareness and self-discovery.

Emotional

The Emotional Discipline is about you and your emotional intelligence. This discipline is concerned with your ability and understanding of how to manage your stress, emotions, and moods and will help you to be an effective person and leader. This discipline focuses on managing life's challenges in a positive, optimistic way by demonstrating self-control, personal fortitude, and moral character. It is about harnessing the power of managing emotions.

Physical

The Physical Discipline is about you and your health. This discipline is concerned with your physical wellness and wellbeing. This discipline focuses on improving your participation in regular physical activities, which improve cardiovascular strength and endurance, flexibility, and muscular strength. This discipline also focuses on your understanding of how your personal wellness and wellbeing effects your personal growth, development, and ability to function daily.

Mental

The Mental Discipline is about your intellectual and mental health capacity. This discipline focuses on your intellectual growth, mental activities, and your creative and critical thinking. This discipline also focuses on healthy brain function as a major component of wellness and peak performance.

Social

The Social Discipline is about your social awareness and social intelligence skills. This discipline focuses on the skills necessary to be accepted and happy socially. This discipline also focuses on developing and sustaining trustworthy, valued relationships and friendships.

Eight Life Qualities

Along with the eight area of self-development eight life qualities that are important to the Unstoppable Model. These proactive life qualities are stepping-stones that will guide you along your journey. Each quality is a way of proactively and positively developing and directing your life to achieve your desired outcomes and achievements.

Each life quality is necessary to live an Unstoppable Life by establishing a solid foundation for an authentic and abundant life. Each life quality concentrates on an aspect of how to live an Unstoppable Life.

The life qualities shape and mold your approach to growing and developing yourself. Each quality has four characteristics that represent the key parts of the life quality.

The combined quality and associated characteristics are key components of the Unstoppable Model and represent the core of an Unstoppable Life.

The number one Unstoppable Life quality is Leadership. You must be able to lead your life through Personal Insight and Personal Mastery in order to achieve your desired end state and life goals.

If you do not lead your life each day then someone else will tell you how to lead it. Leadership allows you to live your life large and to achieve your life goals and dreams. The leadership characteristics are self-leadership, self-control, self-efficacy, and self-discipline. All four characteristics are essential to leading and managing your life. Each characteristic describe a life of leadership and the necessary actions to achieve it.

Life Qualities	Characteristics
Leadership	Self-Leadership Self-Control Self-Efficacy Self-Discipline
Focused	Dedicated Steadfast Persistent Perseverance
Trustworthy	Credible Honesty Integrity Dependable
Resilient	Flexible Adaptive Proactive Agile
Passion	Energy Enthusiasm Drive Motivation
Values-Based	Ethics Morals Standards Principles
Responsible	Accountable Life Ownership In Charge In Control
Transformation	Change Reinvention Growth Development

Summary

Through a disciplined approach you prepare yourself for opportunities that you would not have if you lived life in a laissez faire manner. Through a disciplined approach, you accept responsibility and accountability for your decisions and actions, which allow you the freedom to accept your failures and successes equally.

Live Life Inspired!

REFLECTION TIME

Give yourself some quiet time—20 minutes to start and reflect on who you truly are.

Personal Self-Assessment

Review the questions and select the answer that best fits how you assess your life at this moment.

I use a disciplined approach to my development.

1 2 3 4 5 6 7 8 9 10

I am in control of my life and the path I follow.

1 2 3 4 5 6 7 8 9 10

I continuously grow and develop myself every year.

1 2 3 4 5 6 7 8 9 10

I have good personal insight into my life.

1 2 3 4 5 6 7 8 9 10

My commitment to self-discipline shapes my life.

1 2 3 4 5 6 7 8 9 10

I embrace personal mastery as a part of life.

1 2 3 4 5 6 7 8 9 10

I am passionate about being the best I can be.

1 2 3 4 5 6 7 8 9 10

I seek to develop my inner core.

1 2 3 4 5 6 7 8 9 10

I always exceed expectations in my life.

1 2 3 4 5 6 7 8 9 10

Self-Assessment Analysis

10-39 Points – You need to increase your self-awareness and self-efficacy. Take the time to do a deep dive on yourself to find out who you are and how to improve your life. If you want your life to be a masterpiece, you need to be the master of the pieces of your life.

40-70 Points – You have a good understanding of who you are but have areas that need to grow and develop. Which area of your life do you need to improve? What effects do you need to implement to produce better outcomes?

71-89 Points – You are well on your way to being unstoppable in your life. You are living an abundant life and you understand the Principle of the Harvest. You know your true self and you are living your true purpose. Keep your eye on the prize and keep pressing forward.

90-100 Points – You are unstoppable. You are the Master of the Pieces of your life. However, do not stop now. You need to continue to grow, develop, and continually reinvent yourself.

UNSTOPPABLE TAKEAWAYS
Live Unstoppable

To live an unstoppable life you need to plan and prepare yourself through a disciplined approach. face life's challenges The Unstoppable Model is a disciplined method of self-development and building self-efficacy. It is a way to construct your life to achieve your goals and desires.

ARE YOU BREATHING A.I.R?

Take a moment to reflect on your life. Look at the chart of actions, impacts, and results and use it as a road map to guide you on your Journey. What is your next step in your expedition?

ACTIONS	**IMPACT**
<ul><li>Discipline</li><li>Purposeful</li><li>Change</li><li>Courage</li><li>Commitment</li><li>Proactive</li></ul>	<ul><li>Inspired Life</li><li>Create a future of possibilities</li><li>Actionable</li></ul>
RESULTS	
<ul><li>Unleashed Life!</li><li>Your life is filled with possibilities</li></ul>	

CHAPTER 4
THE INNER CORE
THE REAL YOU

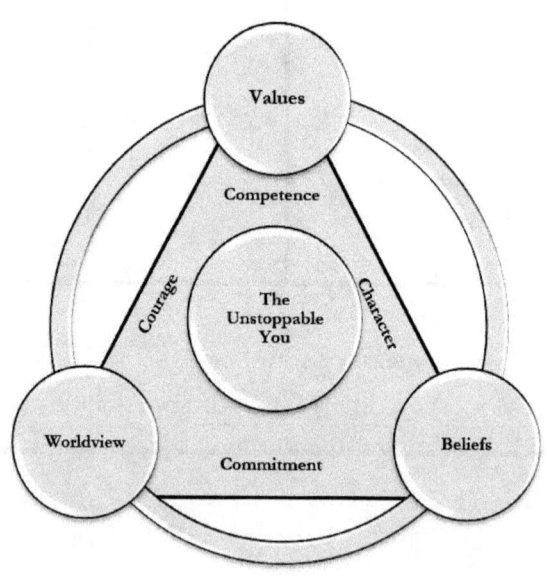

"A journey of a thousand miles begins with a single step."
Lao-tzu

"Write it on your heart that every day is the best day in the Year."
Ralph Waldo Emerson

Discover Your True Self

*"There are three things extremely hard:
steel, a diamond, and to know one's self."*
Benjamin Franklin

It was early on the morning of July 29, 2009, and I was standing on the East Coast Shore of Kwajalein Island looking at the vast expanse of the South Pacific Ocean. Kwajalein Island is the southernmost and the largest of the islands in the Kwajalein Atoll. It is 9.1939° N latitude and 167.4597° E longitude. I had just finished my morning run and stopped to take in the wonder of the morning.

I was awestruck by the beauty of the ocean, the sand, and the sun. The South Pacific water was a deep dark blue and the waves looked like crashing crystals as the sun shone on each undulating wave. The scene was awe-inspiring!

Although I had to be ready in an hour for the helicopter flight to Roi-Namur, I sat down in the sand and took some time to reflect and be quiet. I took a long draw of warm salty air into my lungs and closed my eyes to listen to the sounds that surrounded me--the crash of the waves as they hit the beach, the sounds of sea terns as they flew overhead, and the rustle of the grass as the wind blew.

I was mesmerized and transfixed by the beauty that God created and I was gratefully enjoying it. I took this time to contemplate and reflect on my journey through life thus far. I took the time to reflect on where my life started and where I was that day.

As I sat there assessing my life as a whole and reflecting on what I had accomplished, I realized it was by the Grace of God that I was on this shore enjoying His creation. During my time on the beach, I reflected on Philippians 4:10-13.

> The Lord gives me a reason to be full of joy. It is because you are able to care for me again. I know you wanted to before but you did not have a way to help me. I am not saying I need anything. I have learned to be happy with whatever I have. I know how to get along with little and how to live when I have much. I have learned the secret of being happy at all times. If I am full of food and have all I need, I am happy. If I am hungry and need more, I am happy. I can do all things because Christ gives me the strength.

Through Christ, I can do all things because he provided me the strength and the power to be content in every situation of my life. Through each step and phase of life, I could see the hand of God in each moment of my life.

God blessed me with a great partner for life in my wife Dorene and with three wonderful sons who bring joy into our lives. God also provided the people, opportunities, and challenges in my life that made me the person I am and who I will be in the future.

As my mind raced through a self-reflection and self-awareness of God's blessings in my life, I was shocked into the realization that my life is finite and small in comparison to the vastness and timelessness of the ocean. It struck me that I needed to engage life as actively as possible because life is too short.

It also quickened the desire in my heart, mind, body, and soul to make an impact while I was still alive and to live purposely and meaningfully lest I waste the gift of life God had given me. Our presence on earth is minute in comparison to the time a redwood lives on this earth. We live and then pass on to the ages.

The real question is what do you plan to do with your time? What do you want to accomplish? What do you want to leave behind? Will you waste your time and only be remembered as the obituary in the paper?

On the other hand, will people remember you for your passion for life, your willingness to live authentically, and for the lasting impact you made on their lives?

Each of us is granted a sliver of time on this earth. You have one moment in time to make an impact and to become a person of impact. You need to unleash yourself and become the leader in your life.

After leaving Kwajalein, I reflect on my life at the beginning of each New Year. I take the time to review and recalibrate what I believe about myself—my core beliefs, my worldview, and my core values—to see if I was being true to myself and if I was being an authentic person and leader.

I take the time to make sure I am living in accordance with what I believe and value or if I am living falsely. Are my soul and character congruent, or are they fighting one another? Have my core beliefs changed?

The inner reflection helps me reinforce what I believe, value, and how I see the world. It helps me to live purposefully and meaningfully each year. It allows me to by my true self.

Look around you at people who are wasting their moment in time. They waste their lives through drugs, alcohol, and other life destroying vices. They waste their lives by accepting their fate versus challenging the status quo. They live their lives in fear because they do not want to challenge themselves and try new things.

They do not live their lives to their fullest because they do not want to get out of their comfort zones. How often do you take the time to be quiet, reflect on yourself, and do some soul searching? Most of the time we choose to waste our time with the emptiness fillers of email, TV, or games.

How often do you take the time to contemplate and think about your life, its direction, and the goals you want to accomplish? How often do you allow yourself to drink in the beauty of the day before you start the day?

> Do you really know your true self or have you forgotten what you truly believe in, value, or hold dear? Do you have intentional clarity and focus in your life?

A Focused Life

When I arrived at Vandenberg Air Force Base as the new 14th Air Force "Flying Tigers" Command Chief, I took several months to get to know the people of the Command and learn about my new organization and its organizational culture.

As I traveled throughout the command, I had the opportunity to talk Airmen, Soldiers, Sailors, and Marines that supported the space mission of the Joint Space Operations Center.

A key part of my talks with the young enlisted personnel was about continuously growing, developing, and reinventing themselves. I stressed that they needed to be proactive about their education and training and their personal growth and development so they could achieve their goals.

I asked each of them to think about how to grow and develop themselves in the three growth and development areas of our professional development program--Personal, Professional, or Leadership Competency.

I urged them to invest and reinvest in their life so that they were ready for life's challenges. Furthermore, I asked each person to seek out opportunities, challenges, and resources to help them stretch and get out of their comfort zone.

It was during my visits that I found myself using the well-known colloquialism "6Ps" phrase—"Proper Planning Prevents Piss Poor Performance"—quite frequently. I began to realize how negative and reactive that phrase really was, especially coming from someone talking about being proactive.

The phrase, although technically correct, is a negative and reactive saying and does nothing to help the person who is dealing with the situation.

On my return trip home on the airplane, I started to reshape my use of the 6Ps. I needed a proactive and positive set of 6Ps. I sought out words that described how to proactively shape, live, and forge your life.

After several weeks of thought and talking with peers about the words I selected, my new 6Ps became: Planning, Preparation, Performance, Passion, Persistence, and Perseverance.

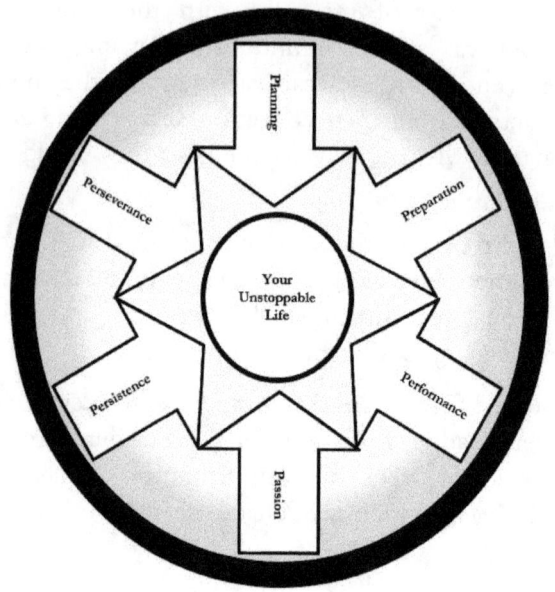

- Planning – To shape your unstoppable life you must know what you want to accomplish to make your dreams your reality. Therefore, the very first step in designing your unstoppable life is to plan it. You need a map and guide to your growth and development and planning that helps you chart the course of your life. You must be consciously committed to a disciplined approach to mastering yourself.

- Preparation – Ben Franklin said, "Failing to prepare is preparing to fail." You must prepare yourself for the journey and prepare yourself for opportunities and challenges. You need to prepare yourself for opportunities and possibilities in life by preparing yourself before they show up in your life. Through training, education, development, and experiences, you prepare yourself for whatever life throws at you.

- Performance – You need to take action and perform to your utmost each day to live unstoppable. Your success in life is not by accident, but by design. You must strive each day to live your life and achieve your goals and dreams. Goals achieve nothing unless you take action. It must be an "all-in" approach to your life--100% of your heart, mind, body, and soul. Nothing else will do in order to achieve your unstoppable life. It is your life…Own it!

- Passion – This is the core power that you have in your life. You must have passion or "fire in your belly" to live unstoppable. Passion is the spark that ignites you each day to live your life to its fullest and on purpose. It is the lynchpin of an inspired and unstoppable life.

- Persistence – You must constantly press forward in life no matter the struggle. You stand in the face of adversity and choose to weather the storm. Persistence is your willingness to keep your eye on the prize and keep moving forward on your journey. Persistence is critical in forging your unstoppable life.

- Perseverance – You must never quit on yourself or your dreams. You must never give in on achieving your dreams. You must never give up on creating the life you want to live. Perseverance is the lodestar of an unstoppable life.

Each of the words became a part of my overall development focus and eventually a part of an unstoppable life. Each of these words help you to create your unstoppable life. The 6P Focus is your daily reminder to grow and develop your life.

The 6Ps are part of the disciplined approach to growing and developing your life. 6P Focus is about choosing where to put your time, passion, attention, and balancing your life priorities. Using the 6P Focus helps you keep your life priorities in order and in the forefront of you daily life.

Why is the 6P Focus important? Because where you put your focus on intentionally, your life will follow. Your day-to-day focus will shape your life. Each day your mind races with your own thoughts, ideas, and intentions while being bombarded with the noise and clutter of the day-to-day issues of work, home, and life. Collectively these things compete for your attention and can cause you to become unfocused and distracted. You can choose to focus on all of these competing issues and matters of you can choose to focus your mind and things that truly matter and are important to create your unstoppable future.

The 6Ps Focus guides you on creating your unstoppable life through six key shaping and molding processes. They help you focus on what you need to do each day to continuously grow, continuously develop, and continuously reinvent your unstoppable life.

The 6P Focus works best if you take 60 minutes at the beginning of each month to review your priorities, goals, and objectives of your life and then 6 minutes each day to review your life strategy to ensure you heading in the right direction.

Strategic Clarity
"Live as on a Mountaintop."
Marcus Aurelius

Strategic clarity is the "Big Picture" of your life. The 6P Focus is a process that engages you in clarifying your priorities by shaping your thinking. When you have intentional clarity you know the why of your life. When you know the why then you can see the possibilities in life and then create a life strategy to make those possibilities a reality. Having intentional clarity gives you 360-Degree perspective in life.

I have travelled across and through the Rocky Mountains several times and the magnificence and majesty of the mountains takes your breath away. Of course, that could be the effect of the higher altitude, too. As you drive toward the Rocky Mountains, they seem to rise out of the earth and reach straight up to the heavens.

Driving up to the Eisenhower Tunnel out of the Denver Valley, you see the peaks of the Rocky Mountains get closer and more majestic. After you pass through the tunnel and under the Continental Divide, you come out the other side and see the valley below. You also can clearly see for miles and miles along the horizon.

Our lives are like that Rocky Mountain journey. We constantly journey from valley to mountaintop experiences. The mountaintop is always the best experience in life because you can see where you came from and where you are going. The mountaintop gives you the opportunity to see clearly and gives you a fresh perspective that the valley cannot provide.

One technique you can use to help put your life into perspective is through a 360-Degree Peak Perspective.

This unique visualization technique helps you to see your life by creating clarity, focus, and foresight in your life.

Picture yourself on a mountaintop and that you can see 360 degrees. You can look down and see the valleys and the deserts below. You can look around and see the cliffs and precipices. You can look out toward the horizon and see clearly from horizon to horizon. Finally, you can see the sky and heavens above you.

From the peak, you can see everything in your life and allows you to gain clarity and perspective. You can see your opportunities and challenges, your obstacles and possibilities, and your roadblocks and options. From the peak, you can see your life challenges in the valley and the deserts below, and the dangers of the cliffs and precipices. From the peak, you can see how roadblocks and options are affecting your life. From the peak, you can review your life and your decisions and decide what effects you need to put in to place to create your possibilities and opportunities.

From the peak, you can gain a fresh perspective about who you are and what you can and will accomplish. As you grow and develop, you need to stop and use a 360-Degree Peak Perspective to gain valuable insight into your life.

Since we live mostly in the valleys of life gaining the 360-Degree Peak Perspective is important. It takes time to sink your character roots deep so that you are well grounded in your core values and core beliefs. Personal development takes time, patience, and experience to develop a solid character and to ingrain your core values.

Life is a Journey

When I imagine life as a journey, I think of the

expedition of Lewis and Clark to the Pacific Ocean, the Earnest Shackleton and the Endurance expedition to Antarctica, and the 20-year odyssey of Odysseus in Homer's *The Odyssey*. All three of these expeditions are indicative of the journey we go through in life.

Life is an expedition of trials, challenges, experiences, setbacks, and successes. It is a time of choices, responses, outcomes, and decisions. It is a time of soul-searching, self-discovery, and developing a new understanding of who you are and what you are capable of doing in life. It is a time of opportunities, possibilities, learning, and development. It is a time of adventure, misfortune, victory, and defeat.

How you travel along your life's journey is up to you. However, on each expedition is the opportunity to grow, develop, and reinvent yourself. You need to convert all your expedition experiences into life lessons and leverage those lessons into how you live each day. The key is to live each day in the same manner you want to finish life. You can live an unstoppable life and finish well by preparing now!

- The best way to live an Unstoppable Life is to prepare and plan your life NOW!

- The best way to live out your Unstoppable Life is through your passion for life and day-to-day performance!

- The best way to maintain your Unstoppable Life is through dogged persistence and perseverance!

My Journey

In May 2006, Colonel Paul Curlett called me and asked if I wanted to be the Command Chief of the 386th Air

Expeditionary Wing and lead Airmen in combat. I was on my way back to the office from watching battlefield training for our deploying Airmen, so I pulled the truck over and talked to him.

During the interview he asked if I had any reservations about conducting the combat mission of our Airmen. My response back to him was, "Sir, the only way I know how to lead is from the front. Our Airmen are going into harm's way danger everyday so the only way we can properly lead them is to be out there with them." After my answer, he told me to pack my bags and get ready to come forward.

I immediately started the combat training required for the position along with our own battlefield Airmen training. I also reached out to Command Sergeant Major Bill High at Fort Sill for leadership guidance and advice along with training at the Fort Sill Power Projection Platform.

I was making sure I was ready to deploy and be an asset to the Combat Airmen versus a liability. All the training was preparing me for the uncertainty of the area of operations.

Then reality hit me in July 2006.

It was while I was preparing to leave for the assignment and finishing the necessary paperwork to finalize my departure that my mortality awareness kicked in. Part of the necessary paperwork that needed to be accomplished was a new will. Now, my wife and I have done wills before, but they were usually an "in the event an accident happens" administrative drill.

Prior to this time, I did not consciously think that I would die. This time it sunk in that I could die. It was an awakening and it made me truly think what if I do not come back? What would happen to my wife and children? What would be their future? What would I miss if I did not come back? Was I ready to meet my Maker?

For me, soul searching was like putting on a Janus Mask and taking a holistic look at my life. I began to review my beginnings and looking forward to the life I still wanted to live. (Janus was the mythical Roman god of beginnings and endings and was depicted with two faces, which looked at the past and the future.) It was a year of self-reflection.

Soul searching is a purposeful way of reconnecting to what is important and what matters in life. It is a conscious, focused, and reflective way to continue your journey of knowing yourself better. Careful self-examination and a sincere willingness to seek ways to improve yourself will provide you a foundation to build your life. There are several methods to help in your soul searching which include prayer, mediation, and visualization techniques.

The first thing you need to do is find a place that you can be still, allowing your mind to rest and reflect. Find a place that you can cut out the noise and distractions of your life and learn to be still. Finding yourself is a journey, not a destination.

Soul Searching

Soul searching is the unearthing of a deeper meaning in your life. Deep within each one of us there is a longing to live a life of significance and legacy. Soul searching is an honest evaluation of what you believe in your very core.

Soul searching is not a 5-minute once a month action. It will require time, solitude, commitment to yourself, and it will require persistence and perseverance.

The most important step you can take is to look in the

mirror, see who you are first, and take steps to fix your problems and issues so your life has meaning and impact. Do not be blinded by your own shortcomings, discover them and then fix them.

Another aspect of soul searching is that it helps you confront your own mortality. It is only when you finally confront the mortal nature of your life that you begin to seek out the meaning of life. This happens when it dawns upon you that you have an expiration date. It also happens when you encounter a situation or event that might bring about that expiration date.

Why is soul searching important? Because when you don't engage in honest self-analysis and proactive corrective measures, you set yourself up for a fall. Soul searching allows you to rise above a life of mediocrity to a life of importance and success.

Prayer

Use the quiet time to pray and focus your heart and mind on the eternal truths of God. Reflect on what you believe about God. The power of prayer is to connect and make deeper your relationship with the Lord. God is our anchor in the midst of all the confusions and storms of our daily lives. Prayer places you in contact with Almighty God.

Prayer opens your eyes to God's purpose for you. It shines light into the darkness of your doubts and your troubles, and enlightens your hopes and your joys. It gives you new ways of seeing your life. Just like the young Soldier who found his passion for life, faith allows you to be stronger and more resilient in your day-to-day struggles. The power of prayer is the continuous renewal of your outlook on life and its meaning.

Meditation

Life is a journey of returning to your beginnings and reflecting on those beginnings and assigning them new meanings in light of what you know now. Use the quiet time to focus inward and find out more about yourself. Use this time to rejuvenate and to reconnect with your soul. Use this time to find meaning. Take this time to contemplate and reflect on your life and where you are today. Focus on what is important in your life, focus on what is true in your life, and focus on the purpose of your life. Focus on your choices, decisions, and outcomes. Reflect on where you have been and where you want to go.

The Influence of the Inner Core

Our inner core influences how we operate in the world. Our values, beliefs, and worldview influence our priorities, decisions, actions, and our behavior. Through the influence of our inner core we prioritize our results.

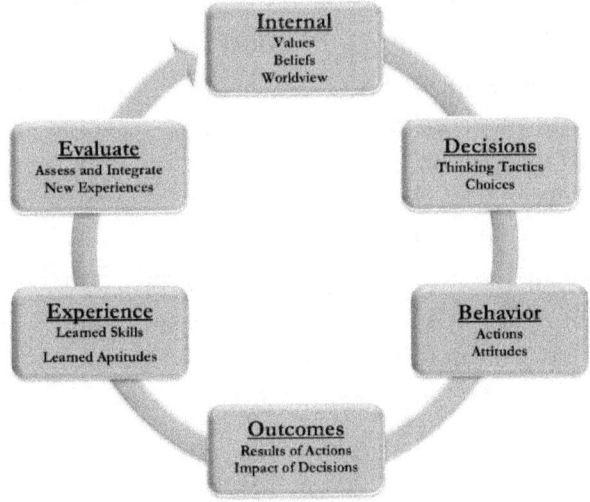

The key to understanding your true self is to know who you are as a person first. What do you believe down deep inside your soul? What do you value in life? What motivates you to be the best person you can be? Knowing your true self makes you more effective in your life.

To understand your true self you need to understand what your beliefs are. You behave according to what you believe, not what you do not believe. A core belief is what your conviction is regarding God, people, concepts, or the world. Your core beliefs are those indispensable elements to defining your life and living it authentically.

Your core beliefs are the center or core of what you believe about life, death, religion, morals, what is good, what is bad, what is right, and what is wrong. Your core beliefs allow you to weather every storm, trial, and tribulation. Being centered in the Truth has become more and more difficult in our society because of relativism and the belief that there is no "right" and "wrong." Core beliefs helps you see what is right and wrong in your life and helps you guide your thoughts and actions.

Core beliefs emanate from your core or your soul. Without solid core beliefs, your personal way of life will be empty and you will be indecisive at every opportunity or challenge in life. The choices you make in life defines who you are as a person.

Your core beliefs define your worldview. Your core beliefs define your core values and shapes your life on a daily basis. Values are those core beliefs that you hold dear, live your life around, and are unchanging. Your core values are shaped by your core belief system.

Values are those things that you hold most dear in your life: family, faith, freedom, human dignity, respect for others, and integrity are just a few examples. These values and beliefs shape your character and shape how you see the world.

Personal values may be aspects of life you think are important to live your life with, such as integrity, excellence, or service. Together these values are the principles that you see your purpose through. Your values drive your behavior and shape your character.

My #1 Core Value

Omni-Integerus—Integrity first, last, and always.

Integrity is more than just a character trait. It is an essential life trait. It is the willingness to do what is right even when no one is looking. It is the "moral compass"—the inner voice; the voice of self-control; the basis for the trust imperative in today's world. The word integrity originates from the Latin *integer* meaning whole, complete, or undivided. The Merriam-Webster dictionary further defines integrity as following a strong moral code.

You cannot survive if you lack integrity or wholeness. President Abraham Lincoln and the Bible (Mark 3:24-25) both indicate that we will experience Cognitive Dissonance when we are incongruent in our lives. **"If a kingdom is divided against itself, that kingdom cannot stand. If a house is divided against itself, that house will not be able to stand."**

A lack of integrity will cause a tension or conflict in your life until you realign yourself to your purpose, values, and beliefs. Authentic people model and maintain their values and act in a way that is both honest and congruent with their beliefs and values.

Integrity is key and essential in military operations and the safe operation of aircraft, ships, and submarines. The integrity or the trustworthiness of a jet fuselage, a ship, or submarine's hull is crucial to safe operations and the survival of the crew.

Integrity in your life means that you intend to live an authentic and true life. Authenticity means a person is accountable and responsible for their actions, words, and decisions.

Character
The greatest unstoppable effect in your life.

Character is the single most important factor in living an Unstoppable Life. Your character is a set of values and beliefs that you live by and define who you are to others. It defines your unstoppable life and profoundly shapes how you engage with the world, how you form your opinions, what you support, what actions you choose to take, and what choices you make.

Character is the outward expression of your purpose, values, and beliefs. Your character is comprised of your beliefs, motives, values, desires, behaviors, and principles that drive and shape your actions as a leader.

Why is it vital for you to reflect on your character each day? Character is a key component of the C4 model. C4 is the most explosive part of the model because it represents who you are deep down inside, your abilities, your strengths, and your passion. These characteristics need to be developed continuously and deliberately.

When you improve your C4, you improve and shape your life. You have control over each of these characteristics in your life. Character, courage, and commitment all start from inside, and your competence is an outward growth of your experiences.

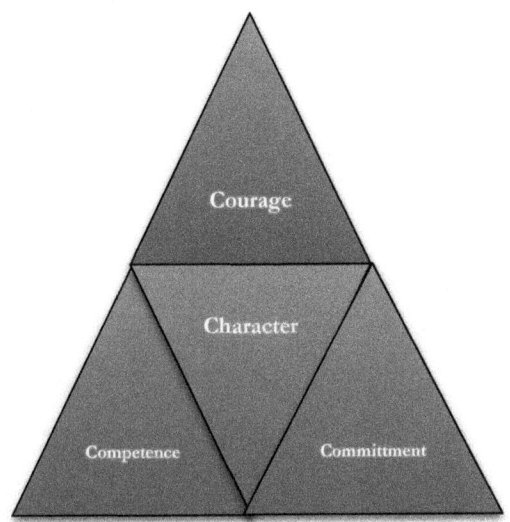

These three components provide you the energy and drive to persevere and persist in life. However, they must remain congruent to your values, beliefs, and worldview to be unstoppable. Nothing is more personal or important than your character. What this means simply is that, if you want to have an Unstoppable Life, you must continually strive to build your character. Your character is your greatest unstoppable effect in your life.

In Shakespeare's play *Hamlet*, Polonius is providing advice to Laertes, "And this above all, to thine own self be true. Then, it must follow as the night the day, thou canst not then be false to any man." You must be your true self and live a genuine and congruent life. To fulfill this statement your inner integrity must shine inside you in order for your integrity to radiate on the outside.

You cannot live two lives if you want to be unstoppable. Living one life is hard enough. When you put on different masks in order to please other people, you separate yourself from your true self, your values, beliefs, and worldview. You start living a lie. Your true life becomes distant and inauthentic. To thine own self be true.

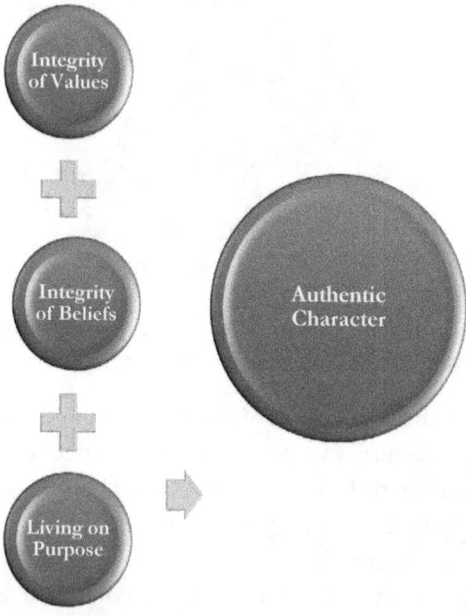

Character authenticity is living on purpose, keeping true to your values and beliefs, and not compromising them at the altar of society. Your character is tested in the crucible of life and is forged through adversity. Your character is important for many reasons. First, without a solid character foundation, the critical link of trust between leaders and followers will not exist. As an authentic leader, your personal integrity should be at the very center of your core. The second value of integrity is your outward expression. You must be trustworthy for people to believe in you. Integrity is the trust factor in life. Integrity refines and defines your character each day. Authentic integrity allows your character to stand the test of time and challenges.

Examine the areas of your life that are not congruent with your purpose. Look for evidence in your life that supports or contradicts your initial thoughts, assumptions, opinions, and beliefs of your life. Adjust your opinions as you reflect on your thoughts and when new information changes your opinion. Don't settle for good enough, achieve your very best, achieve your greatest life. You are living out your true life when you do not compromise your true self

Summary

Discovering your true self is important if you want to live an unstoppable life. The most important undertaking of your life is not what you do, but whom you can and will become. You need to discover the authentic you. When you are living congruent to your purpose, beliefs, and values then you are living authentically. Each discipline provides your life balance, capability, and capacity in all areas of your life. You need to carefully assess your life and understand each of the eight disciplines and how you need to grow and develop in each. By understanding each area, you can strategically design and develop yourself.

Live Life Authentically!

REFLECTION TIME

Give yourself some quiet time—20 minutes to start and reflect on who you truly are.

Personal Self-Assessment

Review the questions and select the answer that best fits how you assess your life at this moment.

The life I lead is a full expression of my true self.

    1 2 3 4 5 6 7 8 9 10

Soul searching is a valuable technique to discover myself.

    1 2 3 4 5 6 7 8 9 10

I use prayer to connect with God.

    1 2 3 4 5 6 7 8 9 10

I use meditation to connect with the inner me.

    1 2 3 4 5 6 7 8 9 10

I take time to get quiet and reflect on my life.

    1 2 3 4 5 6 7 8 9 10

I know what my core values are.

    1 2 3 4 5 6 7 8 9 10

I know my core beliefs.

    1 2 3 4 5 6 7 8 9 10

I know and understand my worldview.

    1 2 3 4 5 6 7 8 9 10

I take time to seek a higher calling.

    1 2 3 4 5 6 7 8 9 10

I want my life to count every day.

    1 2 3 4 5 6 7 8 9 10

Self-Assessment Analysis

10-39 Points – You need to increase your self-awareness and self-efficacy. Take the time to do a deep dive on yourself to find out who you are and how to improve your life. If you want your life to be a masterpiece, you need to be the master of the pieces of your life.

40-70 Points – You have a good understanding of who you are but have areas that you need to grow and develop. Which area of your life do you need to improve? What effects do you need to implement to produce better outcomes?

71-89 Points – You are well on your way to being unstoppable in your life. You are living an abundant life and you understand the Principle of the Harvest. You know your true self and you are living your true purpose. Keep your eye on the prize and keep pressing forward.

90-100 Points – You are unstoppable. You are the Master of the Pieces of your life. However, do not stop now. You need to continue to grow, develop, and continually reinvent yourself.

UNSTOPPABLE TAKEAWAYS

Character Counts

Your character is the outward expression of your values, beliefs, and worldview. The biggest problem today is a lack of character in today's leaders. They say what they want to say in order to keep their leadership position. Unfortunately, when caught in their lies they are not held accountable, or worse, people's livelihood are ruined.

- Refuse to compromise your character
- Refuse to compromise your values
- Refuse to compromise your beliefs
- Refuse to wear a mask to be accepted
- Live your life with integrity
- Live congruent to your values and beliefs
- Live your life honestly and truthfully
- Live your life with courage and trustworthiness

ARE YOU BREATHING A.I.R?

Take a moment to reflect on your life. Look at the chart of actions, impacts, and results and use it as a road map to guide you on your Journey. What is your next step in your expedition?

ACTIONS	IMPACT
• Search your soul • Character building • Values clarification	• Clarity of Self • 360-Degree Perspective

RESULTS
• Authentic Character! • Personal Development Focus

CHAPTER 5

UNSHAKEABLE LIFE PURPOSE

"Success is to be measured not so much by the position that one has reached in life as by the obstacles which he has overcome while trying to succeed."
Booker T. Washington

"Be not afraid of growing slowly; be afraid only of standing still."
Chinese Proverb

Here on Purpose

*"The future you is uncharted territory...explore it.
Let your purpose be your compass and let your principles be
your guiding light."*
Unknown

Too many people compare themselves to people they view as perfect and then waste the rest of their live trying to become that person. The problem with that comparison is "if they are perfect then you are imperfect." You set yourself up for failure because you have established in your mind that you are broken and need to be fixed. I have one word for that kind of madness.

STOP!

You are not broken and you do not need to be fixed. You need quit trying to be perfect in an imperfect world. You are perfect in your own way. You are unique and wonderfully made, so be proud of who you are.

> Instead of spending time trying to create yourself in the image of someone else. Use your time to become the very best YOU.

You are not a mistake. I believe you are a first round draft pick. You are a gift of life. Discovering your purpose in life is part of your journey in life. By living without a purpose in life you wander and get lost because you do not understand what life is all about. Don't self-destruct--find your purpose. Your purpose makes you unstoppable. It provides you with the inner strength and drive to live and lead each day. It equips you with what you need to face the challenges of the day and in life. Your purpose provides context and meaning to your life.

Purpose expresses most deeply, what makes you a unique individual. Your purpose defines who you are, how you live your life, and how you lead. Your purpose is your raison d'etre. Your purpose motivates and drives you throughout life.

Your purpose influences your whole life. Your purpose is the compass that helps you chart your way in the world and in life. Your life and your leadership are driven by one thing...your purpose in life.

I truly believe you are shaped by your purpose in life. Your purpose is the true essence of who you are as a person. Your purpose drives you, influences you, and shapes your actions and reactions to life.

Your purpose is not your career. Your purpose is not what you do. Your purpose defines your character; it is who you are at the center of your core being. There is no escaping who you are.

Your purpose is the embodiment of your heart, mind, body, and soul. It is an amalgamation of your values, your ethics, your core beliefs, your life philosophy, and your worldview.

You need to quit talking yourself into believing what society is telling you that you need to be, and take the time to discover your true self by taking the time to discover your purpose.

You have to believe in yourself. Believing in yourself is a choice even when no one else does. That is what makes you Unstoppable.

My Purpose

The military helped me to define my purpose. The Air Force Core Values helped to truly shape my life. Integrity First…It is a core value every leader should use. Excellence In All We Do…Why would you settle for second best in your life? Service Before Self…A commitment to leading by serving others and a higher purpose.

My purpose in life is to live inspired and to serve and develop other people. This may sound pedestrian, but it is true. My purpose gave me direction, focus, and energy to develop and grow my replacements.

My life purpose defined my life and my career. My belief in Jesus Christ has shaped my purpose. I believe we serve a higher purpose and that we are created equally in God's Eyes. Treating people with respect, dignity, and equally is what we are called to do.

A successful leader needs to be a Servant Leader like Christ, have the Wisdom of Solomon, use the tenacity and management skills of Nehemiah, and be a Son of Encouragement like Barnabas.

Discover Your Purpose

Self-awareness is discovering your purpose and is the key to your success as a leader. How do you discover your purpose? Your purpose is a matter of reflecting on who you are, what excites and motivates you, and what you feel called to do.

Just as you need oxygen to breathe and survive, you need a life's purpose to thrive and survive. Discovering your life's purpose is a process of self-discovery and self-awareness. Part of self-discovery is defining your core values, your beliefs, and worldview. Along with your life's purpose, these are the lenses that you see the world through, handle challenges, and approach your leadership decisions.

The key to harvesting the most out of your life is your willingness to be introspective and reflective as you travel along your expedition. Take time to explore your trials, challenges, and success and take time to savor each experience.

Do a personal deep dive and discover the true meaning from each of these, and carefully examine what you have learned. Use the knowledge you reap from your deep dive to strive to improve how you make decisions, strive to improve your thinking, and strive to improve your true self.

MOMENT OF REFLECTION

After reading the above passages take a moment and ask yourself the following questions. Continue reading when you have answered them honestly.

1. What am I passionate about?
2. What gives me a purpose to live?
3. What excites and ignites me every day to get out of bed?
4. What inspires me to lead every day
5. What is my life's purpose?

L.I.F.E. P.U.R.P.O.S.E.

Adhere to your purpose and you will soon feel as well as you ever did. On the contrary, if you falter, and give up, you will lose the power of keeping any resolution, and will regret it all your life."
Abraham Lincoln

Leadership - Your life purpose begins with the self-knowledge why you are here and what you are living to fulfill. Before you can make an impact on the world, you must make an impact on yourself first by discovering your purpose, your values, and by knowing whom you are. It is an inside-out process and is shaped by your values, character, choices, opportunities, experiences, and your worldview.

Leading with your purpose and your core values ensures your life and leadership are congruent. You are responsible for discovering your life's purpose. Be a role model by living out your authentic leadership daily.

Inspiration - Your life purpose is your daily inspiration for living abundantly. Your purpose excites you, energizes you, and fills you with a great sense of drive and determination. Inspiration empowers and unleashes your life's creativity, innovation, and collaboration.

Living on purpose and serving a higher purpose breathes life into you every day and gives you the desire to reach your goals. You need to live each day congruently by living within your beliefs and values. Unleashing your inspired life starts with living your life purpose. Take time to reflect on an inspirational leader in your life. How did they inspire you and how did it change your life?

Inspiration + Life Purpose = Your Inspired Life

Focus - Your life purpose provides you focus and vision for your life. It is your true north compass and GPS of self-awareness and self-management. Your life purpose is your lens to focus on how your talents, skills, gifts, and abilities will allow you to live on purpose. By focusing each day, you can remove the noise and clutter of life to achieve your life purpose. Your life purpose matters immensely in everything you do. The better you pay attention to your life and life purpose the greater the results.

Your life purpose helps you to focus on your life choices, life opportunities, and life possibilities. Use your focus to discover and analyze your dreams and goals and see if they are congruent with your life purpose. Using your life purpose as your measuring standard, you can create your life vision to achieve your dreams and goals.

Effective - Your life purpose makes your life more effective. Your life purpose enables you to live your life effectively because you know what your life means and what goals you want to achieve. You no longer waste your time on trivial or unproductive things that do not align with your purpose. You stay focused on those actions that will increase your life's potential. A key way you keep your life effective is through goal setting.

The process of setting life affirming goals helps guide you to where you want to go in life. Personal goal setting is a deliberate process for thinking about your unstoppable future and for inspiring yourself to turn your vision of this future into reality. After you have established and set your goals, you need to give each goal a life priority. This will help keep your life effective and efficient and help you to direct your attention to the most important goal first.

Possibilities - Your life purpose provides you with a promise of possibilities. Possibilities are open doors that you can walk through to improve yourself. Each day is a possibility to make an impact and to affect change to fulfill your purpose. Each day is an opportunity to write the next page in your life story and decide to live unstoppable.

Each day begins with a gift of endless possibilities for you to create new life outcomes. The question you need to ask yourself each morning is, "What do I plan to do with this gift of possibility and fulfilling my purpose?" Living within your purpose and on purpose allows you to see the possibilities in your life. It opens your eyes and mind to the positive aspects of your life and the actions you need to take to grab hold of life's possibilities.

Unique - Your life purpose is unique to you and you alone. Your life purpose separates you from others. You are special and unique. You are a unique creation and only you can live out your purpose on earth. You are wonderful and marvelously made and you have a purpose. Each day you need to believe in your unique purpose! Stop for a few minutes to reflect on how unique you are and take time to notice your unique purpose in life.

Even if you are an identical twin, there are minute intricacies that make you unique. Think about it for a minute--you were created for this moment in time. You were created to make a difference and an impact in this world. How you will make a difference will be whether you live on purpose and within your purpose. The key to staying unique is to reject the status quo and take the road less travelled. Live your unique life and unique purpose with passion, enthusiasm, and energy.

Resilience - Your life purpose gives you the flexible spirit to rebound after crisis, chaos, and struggles. Your purpose provides you with the resiliency to face each day prepared. Your purpose provides you with the inner strength each day to press on toward the prize of a life of purpose and fulfillment. Resiliency is keeping strong emotionally, physically, mentally, and spiritually to be fit, healthy, positive, and prepared for all life's challenges. When you have a firm understanding of your life's purpose, you are more resilient to adversity.

When you are living on purpose and within your purpose, you view life's challenges, trials, successes, and setbacks as part of the journey of your life. You are not distracted from your overall vision for your life and you keep on moving forward toward your goals. Seek to be resilient in your life by living purposefully.

Passion - Your life purpose fuels your passion to live and to love. Passion is the burning desire to improve yourself every day and to be the best person you can be in life. Passion is the fire within you! Passion for life is critical to living an unstoppable life. When you are inspired by passion and purpose you are unstoppable and you can do the impossible!

Your life purpose provides you with the drive every day to make your way in the world, regardless of whether you are dealing with an obstacle, setback, frustration, or a great success and joy. You have to LOVE life in order to live unstoppable. You need to be energized and full of life to truly live. Living every day with passion and purpose means you are living your best possible life. Passion and purpose provides you the hope and courage to live greatly each day.

Opportunity - Your life purpose gives you the opportunity to live fearlessly and courageously. Your life purpose allows you to take risks and move beyond your comfort zones. It allows you to break free from your old ways and seek out new opportunities for growth and development. You no longer are seeking your purpose you are living it!

Every day presents you with fresh opportunities to learn, grow, develop, and to reinvent yourself. Look around you and see the great opportunity you have to make a difference in the world. Sometimes just one opportunity can mean the difference between an unstoppable life and a life of mediocrity. We are all capable of seizing life's opportunities each day.

Strength - Your life purpose gives you the strength and courage you need every day to persist, persevere, and overcome life's challenges. Your life purpose is the inner strength you rely on to guide you each day to make decisions and choices. A strong sense of purpose will keep you going strong and help you to overcome when you experience setbacks and failures. If you take the time to live your purpose, you will discover your strength within. Your purpose brings you strength to rise above the noise and confusion of the day, to allow you to see the big picture of your life.

The more you forge ahead in life and use your strength and courage, the more you get to experience your true self! Your life purpose allows you to stop a life cycle of just getting by each day. The strength of your purpose allows you to see opportunities and possibilities of life. Use each day to make the commitment to live each day to your utmost and to be unstoppable.

Empowering - Your life purpose empowers you and enables you to live life abundantly. When you choose to believe in yourself, your life purpose, and your talents, skills, and abilities, anything is possible. Your life purpose unleashes you to live your life and allows you to be unstoppable.

Your greatest power in life is the freedom to choose; you decide what you do, what you think, and where you want to go. No one can take this power away from you; it is yours alone. You can do what you want to do; you can be who you want to be. You can live an empowered life through your decisions and choices each day.

Your choices determine your attitude and your altitude. When you follow a strong and empowering purpose, you will live, think, and act with purpose and within your purpose.

Life Strategy

A life strategy ensures that you have a successful game plan to accomplish your vision and mission. A life strategy consists of four life areas:

(1) your life purpose

(2) your vision and mission statements

(3) your goals, priorities, and objectives

(4) your decisions and actions

Your life strategy is the foundation and guiding principles of a disciplined approach to an Unstoppable Life. Your life purpose is the *why* of your life. It is the raison d'etre of your life. Your purpose influences your whole life. Your purpose is the compass that helps you chart your way in the world and in life. Your life and your leadership are driven by one thing...your purpose in life.

Your vision and mission statements are the *where* and *what* of your life strategy. The vision statement is *where* you want to go in life and defines your end state or life outcomes. Your mission statement is *what* you want to do in the next one, three, five years to move yourself forward to achieving your end states.

Your goals, priorities, and objectives, are the *how* you want accomplish your strategy. You decisions and actions are the *way* you will accomplish your strategy

Envision Your Future

As you continue to develop yourself and your purpose, you need a way to inspire and focus yourself along your journey. Take the time to envision your future. What do you see yourself doing or becoming over the next 3, 5, 15, 30 years?

- **How do you plan to get there?**
- **Do you see yourself as a victor or a victim?**
- **How does your vision fulfill your purpose?**

Life and leadership begin with a clear picture for your life and a vision to fulfill your purpose. Everyone needs a vision in order to know where he or she is going and a plan of how to get there. Vision provides the inspiration and is the starting point for accomplishing your purpose. Vision provides direction for your life. Be bold in defining your life's vision. Your vision for your life will either hold you back or unleash your potential. A clear vision reduces the uncertainty and ambiguity that you will face in life and provides purpose to your life.

- **Your vision describes your future state and is idealistic and ambitious.** Your vision should drive you to a higher standard of personal excellence, challenge you to a higher level of life performance, and motivate you to move beyond the status quo. Your vision should stretch your life from the "as-is" to the "to-be."

- **Your vision clarifies your purpose and mission in life.** Your vision should clarify your life purpose and make clear how you want to fulfill your purpose. Your vision also provides the motivation for your mission statement and the goals you want to achieve. The vision provides context to your life.

- **Your vision encourages, inspires, and energizes you to act.** Your vision should inspire you, fill you with enthusiasm, encourage your full commitment to achieve the vision, and energize you to take action to fulfill your vision. Your vision should make an impact on how you live your life and what you need to do to live your life to the fullest.

A clear and bold vision also creates action. It is the impetus for you to achieve your purpose and life's goals. Without a vision, you are driving blind in life. Worse yet, without a vision, you will waste valuable time and energy trying to achieve your purpose. Why? Because everything you end up doing will be an experiment versus intentional.

Visualization

One technique to help you envision your future life is a technique called visualization. Visualization is a technique to help you create a mental image or intention of what you want to happen or feel. By using visualization, you can mentally picture what your future could look like. In effect, you can use it to help you produce your desired outcome in life.

If you watch the Olympics, you will see many of the athletes use visualization techniques prior to their performance. Watch skiers, snowboarders, or ice skaters just prior to their turn. Their eyes are closed and they are mentally walking through their performance.

They visualize accomplishing their routine and see themselves land every jump, twist, and flip before they ever set foot on the snow or ice. A great competitor knows where to go in their mind to create a great performance.

You can do anything your heart and mind agree on if you believe in paying the price, are committed to the necessary hard work, and believe in yourself completely. I encourage you to dream big with your vision. Do not limit yourself, visualize what you can become, what you want to achieve, or what you want to do.

Big dreams are a part of an unstoppable life. You need to open the aperture of your mind and see your life with a new perspective. By dreaming big, you open the door to a life of possibilities. Your life's vision should excite you and inspire you. It should set you on fire and fuel your passion to achieve it.

Your vision should move you from your "as-is" life to the "to-be" life. Take your time and focus on a clear and positive future. Close your eyes and see your life like a movie in which you are in the starring role. Imagine for a moment that you see your future self.

- **What do you see?**
- **What do you feel?**

- **What are you doing?**
- **What have you accomplished?**
- **What does your life look like?**

Take a moment and watch your future unfold. Focus on who you want to become, where you want to live, what impact you want to make, and what you want to give back to your community.

Envision what your family life could be, what career you could have, and what places in the world you want to see. Give yourself enough time to visualize your life's vision, then write it down.

Writing it down will help you capture your dream and will help you turn it in to reality. After you know what your future can look like it is time to start making it a reality.

Vision and Mission Statement

Why do you need a personal vision and mission statement? Personal vision and mission statements bring clarity and a laser focus to your life. In this book, you have learned the answer to your purpose. Your life purpose answers the question of "why?" you are here. It is your reason for being.

A vision statement isolates "what you want to accomplish" while you are here. A mission statement specifies "the method" you want to use to accomplish your purpose.

A vision is a rich, vivid, and captivating mental picture of the life you want to create. It should excite you and motivate you to live. Your personal vision statement is a strategic or "big picture" view of your life.

This statement is for you to use as a constant reminder of where you are going in life and what is important. It is part of the inside-out look of the F(X) process by examining your life. The first person you need to inspire is yourself. A personal vision statement is a vision of whom you want to become.

After you develop your vision, your next step is to translate your purpose and vision into a personal vision and mission statement.

Your personal mission statement is what you plan to do to achieve your vision. Writing your mission statement begins by focusing on your values, your life's philosophy, your purpose, talents, skills, and your guiding principles.

A personal mission statement is not a one-time event, but an evolving process. As you grow and develop as a person, your mission statement will change. Your mission statement crystallizes your life. As you continue to develop yourself and your purpose, you need a way to inspire and focus yourself along your journey.

The vision and mission statements help you to implement your well-defined life and leadership goals. Having a personal vision and mission statement is a tangible method to write down your vision, purpose, and long-term and short-term life goals. Goals refer to "how you plan to accomplish" specific goals to the actions and results needed to complete their mission and realize their purpose.

It is about moving from the "as-is" life to the "to-be" life. It is a critical look at what you want to become and what kind of future life you desire. Your personal vision should excite and inspire you to act on your vision through your mission statement.

Summary

Do you see yourself as limited by your potential or limitless by your opportunities? Are you ready to unleash your leadership and change your life? If you wake up full of energy every day, focused and ready to live abundantly, you probably have identified, and are living your life's purpose and have a vision for your life. Seek out the possibilities in your life.

Live Life On Purpose!

REFLECTION TIME

Give yourself some quiet time—20 minutes to start and reflect on who you truly are.

Personal Self-Assessment

Review the questions and select the answer that best fits how you assess your life at this moment.

I know my life's purpose.

    1 2 3 4 5 6 7 8 9 10

I am living my life's purpose.

    1 2 3 4 5 6 7 8 9 10

Life is an expression of my life's purpose.

    1 2 3 4 5 6 7 8 9 10

I live true to my life's purpose.

    1 2 3 4 5 6 7 8 9 10

My life reflects my life's purpose.

    1 2 3 4 5 6 7 8 9 10

I have a vision for my life.

    1 2 3 4 5 6 7 8 9 10

My vision guides me to fulfill my life's purpose.

    1 2 3 4 5 6 7 8 9 10

I have a purpose statement for my life.

    1 2 3 4 5 6 7 8 9 10

I have a vision and mission statement for my life.

    1 2 3 4 5 6 7 8 9 10

Self-Assessment Analysis

10-39 Points – You need to increase your self-awareness and self-efficacy. Take the time to do a deep dive on yourself to find out who you are and how to improve your life. If you want your life to be a masterpiece, you need to be the master of the pieces of your life.

40-70 Points – You have a good understanding of who you are but have areas that you need to grow and develop. Which area of your life do you need to improve? What effects do you need to implement to produce better outcomes?

71-89 Points – You are well on your way to being unstoppable in your life. You are living an abundant life and you understand the Principle of the Harvest. You know your true self and you are living your true purpose. Keep your eye on the prize and keep pressing forward.

90-100 Points – You are unstoppable. You are the Master of the Pieces of your life. However, do not stop now. You need to continue to grow, develop, and continually reinvent yourself.

UNSTOPPABLE TAKEAWAYS
Live Fearlessly

Don't sell yourself short, you only get one chance to make a difference and an impact. Take the time and envision where you want to be 5, 10, and 20 years from now, then put your plan in to action and achieve your dream! No matter where you are in your life right now, you have the power to transform your life!

Discover Your Purpose

The first thing you need to do is to awaken the leader within you. It is about discovering your true purpose. It is about seizing control of your life by discovering your purpose. To be an effective and successful person you need to figure out what is important to you, what matters in your life, and what you stand for. You need to live out your purpose authentically and daily. You need to passionately pursue your purpose in life and relentlessly challenge yourself to become better.

ARE YOU BREATHING A.I.R?

Take a moment to reflect on your life. Look at the chart of actions, impacts, and results and use it as a road map to guide you on your Journey. What is your next step in your expedition?

ACTIONS	IMPACT
• Discovery • Envision • Visualize • Passion • Focus	• Purpose Discovery • Create a Life Vision • Daily Inspiration
RESULTS	
• Your life is not a mistake! • Inspiring Vision for your Life	

CHAPTER 6
THE OUTER RINGS
DEEP DIVING INTO YOUR LIFE

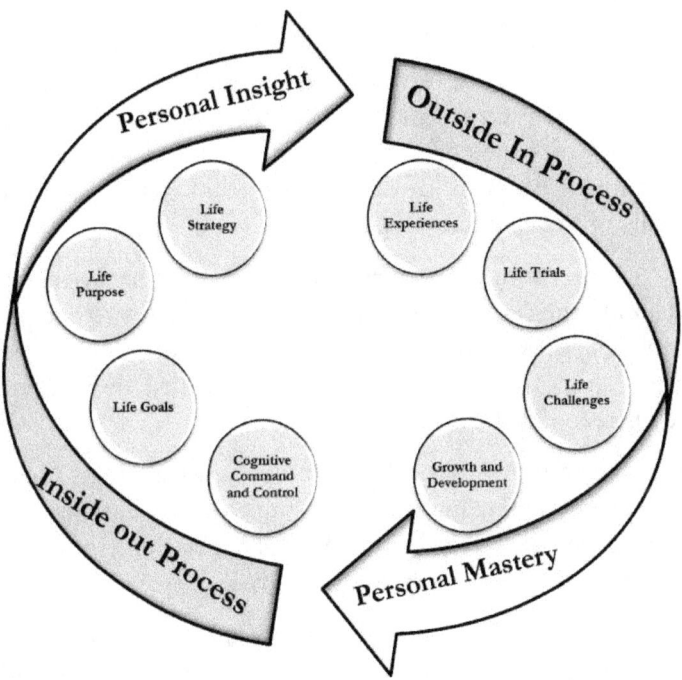

"Life's a forge - Yes, and hammer and anvil, too. You'll be roasted, smelted, and pounded, and you'll scarce know what's happening to you. But stand proudly to it. Metal is worthless till it is shaped and tempered. More labor than luck. Face the pounding, don't fear the proving; and you'll stand well against any hammer and anvil."

Lloyd Alexander

Create a Masterpiece

Envision yourself sitting at an old potter's wheel with a lump of clay on the wheel head. You begin to work the foot pedal, the wheel turns and the clay rotates. Your hands surround the clay and you can see the potential of the clay. You can see the beautiful vase that lies in this dormant lump of clay.

You see the beauty and life within. You start to apply pressure to even the clay out and to force it to take form. As you work the core of the clay you start to form a hole. With each new turn of the wheel the hole widens and the walls of the clay start to take shape.

You continue to turn the wheel, you begin to add water to the clay as you turn and the vessel starts to become smooth and look finished. With the final turn of the wheel, the shape of the vessel begins to be revealed and the true art is recognized.

The true worth and beauty of the vase has not been achieved yet. The master artisan puts the clay vase into the kiln to be fired, tested, and cured. The vase emerges from the kiln and now is a thing of beauty.

You can fill the vase up with whatever you want it to hold. Just as the master artisan creates a masterpiece with the clay, you are creating a masterpiece as you grow and develop yourself. The true art is your life.

Your purpose, values, and worldview guides your hand as the clay rotates around the wheel and molds and shapes your life. The kiln represents the trials, challenges, and successes of life that temper you and forge your life.

It is an Awakening when you realize that you are the owner of your own solution…Build your Masterpiece!

- Look for cracks in your life before you leave the potter's wheel
- Look for impurities in your character before you are tested by trials and challenges
- Face your fears while you are being tested so you emerge fearless
- Understand that you are responsible for your life
- You are responsible for your growth and development
- Seek to achieve mastery of your life and leadership to lead and dare greatly
- Life is a performance art, so create a masterpiece out of your life
- Take time to discover who you really are
- You are unique, there is no one like you
- Invest in your capabilities
- Invest in your talents
- Invest in your character

Forge Ahead or Fall Behind

A great part of my job during my time in the military was the one-on-one counseling meetings with young enlisted personnel called first-term Airmen. As an opening to our counseling session, I traditionally asked them, "Why are you here?" For the most part the Airmen had a clear answer for joining the Air Force.

"I joined for the education."

"I joined because my father/mother was in the Air Force."

"I joined to see the world."

"I joined to serve my Country."

"I joined to do something with my life."

The next five questions after I understood **WHY** they joined the Air Force stumped many of the Airmen. The five questions after the why were:

- Who are you?
- What do you want to become?
- Where do you want to end up in life?
- How do you plan to achieve your end state?
- When do you plan to start changing your life?

Ninety percent of their answers were vague or ambiguous and lacked the concreteness of purpose to achieve what they envisioned for their life.

The Airmen answered the why question with confidence and clarity because they knew why they were there. Unfortunately, most of the Airmen struggled with the other questions because they did not take the time to think and plan their future past the present.

As the conversation continued, I informed them: You need to forge ahead or you will fall behind in life and in the

Air Force. I need you to be engaged every day in developing your skills, talents, and capabilities to help us to achieve our mission in the Air Force. However, you need to be engaged with your life every day so you can achieve your purpose, vision, and goals in life.

At the end of the counseling session, each Airman had a homework assignment due to me in a month—to answer the five questions completely and bring the answers back to me. Through this technique, I helped several Airman design a life action plan with goals and outcomes. This process eventually became what I call the FORGE Process.

The FORGE Process

Forging a life is hard work and requires dedication and commitment to bettering oneself. It also requires endurance and perseverance to go through the refiner's fire of life and emerge victorious. The art of forging was and is a metalworking and sword-making process that heated steel to a temperature that the blacksmith could manipulate and shape to create an object or sword.

In ancient times forging was performed by a blacksmith using hammer, anvil, and hearth to increase the metal strength through a process of heating, hammering, reheating, and shaping.

The sword-making process of folding the steel was made by repeatedly heating, hammering, reheating, and folding the metal into itself several times to improve strength, remove impurities, and create a masterpiece.

Before the sword was forged, it was a concept or vision in the blacksmith or sword-makers head. The vision of the sword was then sketched out and the sword design was realized. After the design was complete, a detailed plan was developed to produce the work of art. This plan detailed each step, the necessary resources, and the timeline for development.

The F(X) FORGE Process details the effects that you need to put in your life to change or direct the outcomes. It is a way of thinking about the 2nd, 3rd, and 4th order of effects that can happen and asking the "what ifs" of your life and preparing yourself for the future.

The FORGE Process is a detailed and proactive way of thinking about your life and its direction. It is a forward thinking model focusing on your end-state goals and the effects that are required to achieve your desired outcome and to produce a masterpiece of your life.

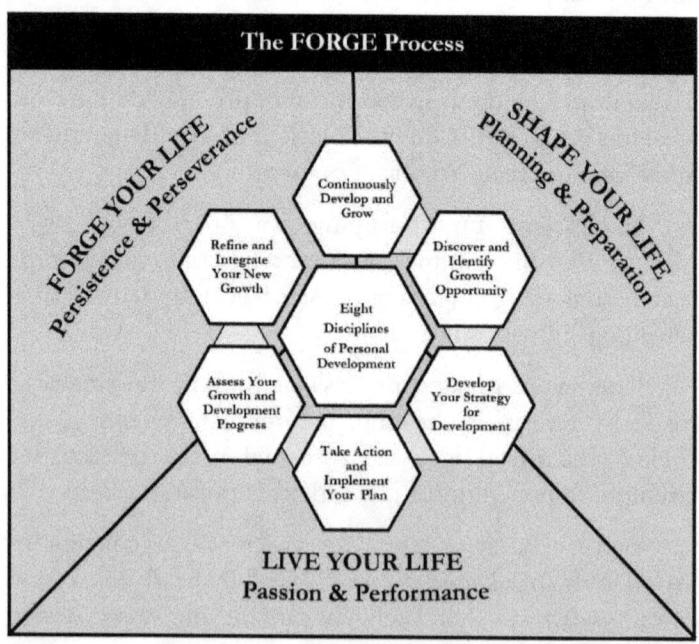

The FORGE Process model has three distinct areas of growth and development.

- The outside area contains the three phases of the Forge Process. The first phase is **SHAPE YOUR LIFE** and is the planning and preparation phase of your life. This phase is about knowing who you are, what you are capable of doing, and what actions you need to do to shape your unstoppable life.

- The second phase is **LIVE YOUR LIFE** and is the passion and performance phase of your life. This phase is about the passion, enthusiasm, and energy you have in life and how well you are living your unstoppable life. This is the execution phase of your life plan and you begin to move from the "as-is" to the "to-be" you.

- The third phase is **FORGE YOUR LIFE** and is the persistence and perseverance phase of your life. This phase is about reevaluating your growth and development life's strategy, incorporating new growth in your life, and pressing forward in living your unstoppable life.

The next part of the FORGE Process is the inner circle of the model. The circle contains the six elements of developing your life's strategy and life plan. The six elements are:

- Continuously Develop and Grow
- Discover and Identify Growth Opportunity
- Develop Your Strategy for Development
- Take Action and Implement Your Plan

- Assess Your Growth and Development Progress
- Refine and Integrate Your New Growth

Discover and Identify Growth Opportunity

The six-element process begins with the Discover and Identify Growth Opportunity stage, which requires self-awareness. Do you know all your talents, gifts, opportunities, and capabilities? Do you know what growth opportunities you need to develop you for future challenges?

The first step in building your self-awareness is self-assessment. Use self-assessment exercises to help you in the transformative process. Using self-assessment exercises can help you to discover and identify your areas of growth opportunity.

Develop Your Strategy for Development

Once you can answer these questions, you can move on to the Develop Your Strategy for Development. This stage is where you develop your life change strategy to grow in those areas of opportunity you have discovered and identified.

Your strategy must focus on the desired effects, future states, or outcomes you want to develop or change in the next year. Your strategy is your tactics, techniques, and procedures you will implement to achieve your desired outcomes.

This is the true essence of F(X) leadership. What do you need to do to create the effects or outcomes in your life or leadership that you desire?

Take Action to Implement Your Plan

This stage is where the actual execution of the growth and development strategies take place in order for change to happen. Below is an example of a developmental plan.

<u>12-Month Life Plan</u>

I. Personal – Inspiring My Self
- Live my life Authentically
- Choose to live on purpose and take control of my life
- Choose each day to be awake and alive
- Choose each day to Inspire

II. Professional/Technical – Creating Capacity in My Life
- Seek one new career improvement opportunity through advanced education and/or professional certification
- Mentor subordinates quarterly to increase their career knowledge
- Develop two new strategic alliances in the organization to increase my organizational leadership
- Attend two career development workshops

III. Emotional – Overcoming Fear and Controlling My Emotions
- Learn more about Emotional Intelligence so I have the ability to express and control my own emotions
- Take an Emotional Intelligence Competence Inventory
- Take each fear in my life and discover how to tackle them one step at a time

IV. Mental – Building Resiliency
- Live my life in balance: Spiritual, Social, Physical, and Emotional
- Build more positive thinking in to my life
- Learn to be more flexible and adaptive to life
- Keep my life's challenges in perspective

V. Social – Sharing My Life
- Participate in a local community group to help take care of our playgrounds
- Develop a solid social network in the local community and my church
- Take a course on communication skills
- Build relationships on trust and respect

VI. Physical – Building My Physical Self
- Participate in a year-long physical fitness program to improve my physical well-being
- Develop an aerobic and an anaerobic routine to build strength and cardiovascular health
- Create a food plan to incorporate healthy foods into my daily intake
- Reduce sugar and gluten in my daily food intake

VII. Spiritual – Discovering God
- Go back to church
- Read the Bible every morning to connect with God
- Use meditation to find my inner voice
- Pray and be still with God

VIII. Leadership – Building and Discovering Self
- Take a personal assessment this year to improve self-awareness (i.e., DISC, MBTI, Big Five, CPI 260 Instrument)
- Participate in a leadership seminar this year
- Request leadership feedback from my mentor

Assess Your Growth and Development Progress

The assessment stage focuses on the impact of the change by assessing the results of the effects on your daily life. This is your map and compass stage. This stage is also where you assess your plan's effectiveness against the milestones and timelines you have laid in the plan. By continually assessing your life's progression, you know where you are going and how you know when you get there.

Refine and Integrate Your New Growth

This stage is where your change strategies are implemented to produce new levels of knowledge of self-awareness. This stage is where all your hard work has paid off. Your outcome has been achieved and you have acquired a new skill, talent, or mindset to help you continue to grow and develop in your growth areas.

Continuously Develop and Grow

This stage is where you begin to evaluate yourself again to find out what other skills, talents, or mindsets you need to acquire after you have grown in an area. Using the FORGE Process you can grow and develop yourself and become a better leader.

Goals, Objectives, and Actions

The purpose of setting a goal is to change your life in a positive way. Goals are a way to manage your growth and development as a person and help you manage the change. Your life would be stagnant without personal change. Your life would be like the aircraft sitting on static display—unrealized potential and energy.

You need goals that are realistic, laser-focused, and life-stretching in order to stay driven and inspired. It is up to you to decide how much risk you are willing to accept to achieve your goals.

Goals and objectives need to raise your expectations for your life and make the most of the skills, gifts, and talents you have. You need to set your goals and objectives continuously throughout your life so that you recognize what you are trying to achieve, where you are going, and how well you have accomplished your vision.

Finally, actions are the driving force that allow you to meet your objectives. Action is the force that changes your goals from a dream to a reality.

Goals are the milestones of your lifelong journey, not the endpoints. Objections and actions are the means you use to attain your goals.

Your goals provide you with an opportunity for change, development, and growth and are focused on the long-term. Goals are a statement of personal intent.

- Goals are an essential part of life
- Goals develop and grow you
- Goals provide focus and direction
- Objectives identify desired outcomes
- Actions provide a sense of accomplishment

Objectives are short-term, specific, and actionable statements that tell you what, when, and how you plan to achieve your goals. Your objective must be achievable while at the same time it should make you stretch, grow, and change. The goal setting process begins after you have established your purpose and vision. Begin the process by asking yourself, "What do I need to do this year in order to fulfill my purpose and achieve my vision?"

Next, identify your objectives by contemplating each goal. Ask yourself,

- What must I do to reach this goal?
- What new skills, talents or knowledge are essential?

These questions identify your objectives and actions required to achieve the goal. A beginning step in setting personal goals is to consider what you want to achieve in your life.

The whole point of setting goals, after all, is to achieve them. It does you no good to think of goals without acting on them or completing them. Unfortunately, this scenario describes what far too many people do after setting goals.

- Writing down your goals is a first step toward achieving them. Writing down your goals helps to solidify and establish them as a reality you want to achieve versus a desire of the heart. When you write a goal down it helps to provide you with the necessary concreteness of goal establishment and makes the goal reality-based.
- Ensure you set achievable goals. Goals need to stretch and grow you but they still need to be within your ability and capability. As experience, achievement, and self-assurance develop then you can set your sights on an even higher goal to attain.

- Developing sound goals is critical to managing your life. Each year you should establish and write down your goals. I use the S.MA.R2.T model for establishing goals and objectives. The S.MA.R2.T. or Specific, Measurable, Attainable, Relevant/Realistic and Time-Bound model is a structured tool that allows for a critical analysis of goals and how to achieve them.

S.MA.R2.T Goals

SPECIFIC

Specific means the goal needs to be as concrete as possible. Why do you want to achieve and accomplish the goal? Be as specific as possible to reduce ambiguity. Example: I want to improve my leadership skills by attending leadership seminars this year.

Begin with the end in mind and visualize your goal achievement. Envision yourself reaching your goal. See the outcome of your goal and the effect it will have on your life. Taking the time to picture the results of your desired goal will provide you with the urgency and the energy to accomplish the goal. You will stay motivated to work toward your goal when you envision the desired outcome.

MEASURABLE

A measurable goal is tangible and quantifiable. Example: I want to improve my leadership skills by attending three leadership seminars this year. Outcome-oriented goals mean that you will accomplish an activity that produces outcomes and results. A goal is just a dream on a piece of paper until action is applied. Then it is on its way to becoming a reality. Example: I will attend three leadership seminars this year to improve my leadership skills.

ACTION-ORIENTED

Action-oriented goals mean that I will accomplish an activity that produces outcomes and results.. Why do you want to achieve and accomplish the goal? Be as specific as possible to reduce ambiguity. Your goal needs to be as measurable and specific as possible so that you can evaluate your progress.

This will enable you to know when you have achieved your goal. The final attribute of effective goals are that they are specific. To keep your efforts on track you need to document your goals in clear terms and explain how you intend to achieve them. Example: I want to improve my leadership skills by attending leadership seminars this year.

R^{2}EALISTIC/RELEVANT

Realistic and relevant goals are challenging but achievable and motivate you because they are important to you. Realistic and relevant goals are important to your growth and development requirements because they challenge you to grow and develop. You need to establish goals that excite, energize, and motivate you to succeed.

TIME-CONSTRAINED

Time constrained means there is a definable and a finite period of completion. The goal line mindset is an understanding of where you want to be at goal completion. In order for you to take action on your goal, you need to establish a schedule of completion that provides a realistic amount of time for you to achieve the goal. The schedule must have enough time for you to reach the goal, but not too much time that you lose interest in it.

Expressed Positively

Whatever your goal is, it should be expressed in clear and well-defined terms. You need to have an inspiring goal to help you stay motivated. Ideally, you should set a goal for yourself that requires you to grow and develop as you progress toward your objective. Imagining the positive result of your efforts can help to motivate you even further. This technique can encourage you to persevere when facing obstacles to your goal. A positively expressed goal provides you with the enthusiasm and passion to complete the goal.

Assess Your Progress

Periodically review your focus. A periodic review of your goals will help ensure that they continue to be realistic, relevant, and on their way to achieving your desired outcome. The goal review will help you decide if you want to change the goal or refocus or refine the outcome of the goal.

Identify Roadblocks and Obstacles

As you progress through your goals you will encounter roadblocks and obstacles that will try to deter and inhibit your goal accomplishment. To deal with roadblocks and obstacles, determine what effects you need to put in your life to create the desired outcome.

Identifying the roadblocks and obstacles is imperative for continued growth and development.

Internal roadblocks and obstacles can be your inner thoughts, your worldview lens, your values, and your personal beliefs. Those internal controls or lenses can inhibit your growth and development progress. You need to understand the effect they have on you both good and bad. You have the power to change, alter, or accept your inner roadblocks and obstacles.

External roadblocks and obstacles are circumstances or situations outside your sphere of influence that can prevent you from achieving your goals and objectives and stop your actions from achieving your vision. It is a waste of time and effort to worry over these roadblocks and obstacles.

Eight Disciplines of Goal Setting

Setting life-effecting goals provides you with a global outlook that shapes your decision-making ability. To get a comprehensive, balanced study of all-important areas in your life, you need to set goals in the following eight disciplines of personal growth to improve your life.

- **Emotional** – What fears do you want to overcome? What do you want to learn in order to control or manage your emotions? What steps are you going to take to achieve this?

- **Spiritual** – What do you want to study, explore, or practice about spiritualism, your faith, or another religion? What steps are you going to take to achieve this? How will this help you to build resiliency into your life?

- **Social** – What do you currently do for your community? Are you part of a volunteer organization or do you volunteer your time to help others? How many hours per week do you volunteer? What steps are you going to take to achieve this?

- **Personal** – What do you want to do to learn to express yourself authentically? What do you need to do to pursue new friends and encounter new people? What do you want to do to enjoy your family relationships more? What steps are you going to take to achieve this?

- **Professional/Technical** – What do you want to reach in your career, or what do you want to achieve in your profession? What steps are you going to take to achieve this?

- **Mental** – Is there any specific information or knowledge you want to gain? What development and growth skills do you want to gain? What new mindsets do you want to develop that will help you in your life? What steps are you going to take to achieve this?

- **Physical** – What are the health/physical goals you want to achieve? What healthy habits do you need to incorporate into your life? What steps are you going to take to achieve this?

- **Leadership** – What leadership skills do you need to develop? What teambuilding skills do you need to develop? What inventories or assessments do you need to take to discover your leadership development needs? What steps do you need to take to determine this?

Summary

The FORGE Process is a proactive way of determining what effects you need to put in your life to change or direct the outcomes. It is about taking control of your life and creating the effects you need to create the outcomes you desire. A personal development plan is a roadmap of where you want to go in life. It allows you to express your vision for your life and to define your specific goals and objectives. You must commit yourself to continually forging your life through developmental actions.

Live Life Empowered!

REFLECTION TIME

Give yourself some quiet time—20 minutes to start and reflect on who you truly are.

Self-assessment

Review the questions and select the answer that best fits how you assess your life at this moment.

I believe in my capability to create outcomes for my life.
   1 2 3 4 5 6 7 8 9 10

I want to create a masterpiece of my life.
   1 2 3 4 5 6 7 8 9 10

I am ready to implement the effects I need to change.
   1 2 3 4 5 6 7 8 9 10

I have established personal goals for my life.
   1 2 3 4 5 6 7 8 9 10

I have learned to take a proactive approach to my life.
   1 2 3 4 5 6 7 8 9 10

I am willing to pay the price to create a positive life.
   1 2 3 4 5 6 7 8 9 10

I have established goals in all eight disciplines.
   1 2 3 4 5 6 7 8 9 10

I willingly assess all areas of my life each year.
   1 2 3 4 5 6 7 8 9 10

I know my roadblocks and obstacles.
   1 2 3 4 5 6 7 8 9 10

I am ready to use a disciplined approach to my life.
   1 2 3 4 5 6 7 8 9 10

Self-Assessment Analysis

10-39 Points – You need to increase your self-awareness and self-efficacy. Take the time to do a deep dive on yourself to find out who you are and how to improve your life. If you want your life to be a masterpiece, you need to be the master of the pieces of your life.

40-70 Points – You have a good understanding of who you are but have areas that you need to grow and develop. Which area of your life do you need to improve? What effects do you need to implement to produce better outcomes?

71-89 Points – You are well on your way to being unstoppable in your life. You are living an abundant life and you understand the Principle of the Harvest. You know your true self and you are living your true purpose. Keep your eye on the prize and keep pressing forward.

90-100 Points – You are unstoppable. You are the Master of the Pieces of your life. However, do not stop now. You need to continue to grow, develop, and continually reinvent yourself.

UNSTOPPABLE TAKEAWAYS

Create a Masterpiece of Your Life

Developing yourself requires hard work and creative thinking. Your life is a blank canvas ready for you to begin your artwork. Make it a Rembrandt or a Picasso. The choice is yours.

Forge Your Life and Future

Clear your path of growth and development from roadblocks and obstacles. Roadblocks and obstacles are both internal and external and you may or may not have control over the effects of the roadblocks and obstacles.

ARE YOU BREATHING A.I.R?

Take a moment to reflect on your life. Look at the chart of actions, impacts, and results and use it as a road map to guide you on your Journey. What is your next step in your expedition?

ACTIONS	**IMPACT**
<ul><li>Forge</li><li>Visualize</li><li>Goal Setting</li><li>Develop Yourself</li><li>Grow Yourself</li></ul>	<ul><li>Life Direction</li><li>Change Outcomes</li><li>New Perspective</li></ul>
RESULTS	
<ul><li>Your Life is a Masterpiece</li><li>Forging Your Unstoppable Future</li></ul>	

CHAPTER 7

YOU REAP WHAT YOU SOW

"And there were always choices to make. Every day, every hour, offered the opportunity to make a decision, a decision which determined whether you would or would not submit to those powers which threatened to rob you of your very self, your inner freedom; which determined whether or not you would become the plaything of circumstance, renouncing freedom and dignity to become molded into the form of the typical inmate."
Viktor Frankl

A Parable of the Farmer and Life

"The greater danger for most of us lies not in setting our aim too high and falling short but in setting our aim too low, and achieving our mark."
Michelangelo

During my time in the Air Force and as the Command Senior Enlisted Leader for United States Strategic Command, I had the opportunity to talk to numerous enlisted Soldiers, Marines, Sailors, and Airmen about growing and developing themselves.

Sometimes the talks occurred in my office as part of a one-on-one session to get to know the new enlisted person and welcome them to the unit. And sometimes it occurred in auditoriums as I travelled to see different units globally.

Through my talks I tried to impress upon them that life was a journey, a marathon, and they needed to take the time to invest in themselves for the long haul. Their time wearing the uniform was just a part of their life's journey and they needed to continue to grow, develop, and reinvent themselves for the duration of the journey.

I stressed the importance of becoming the best possible version of themselves that they could become to live a full and abundant life. One of the stories I used during my talks was the Parable of the Farmer and Life.

As we moved to different bases with the military we lived in several agriculturally rich places. Several of the houses we lived in were next to farmers and their fields and in several locations we befriended ranchers and farmers. This talk grew out of those experiences.

Have you ever watched a farmer to see how he takes care of his land? Have you ever watched a field as it grows? Have you ever stopped to wonder how a plant grows in the field prior to it being harvested? An amazing process begins with the farmer.

The Soil

One of the first things you can learn from a farmer is that his life, livelihood, and the land are one. He understands that the soil is an ecosystem and must be nurtured. He takes care of the land and the soil by crop rotation, nutrient cycling, water regulation, and at times, growing nothing to allow the soil to recover so it is ready to grow again the next year.

He takes care of the soil and the land because he knows it will take care of him. Fertile soil ensures growth and life. He understands what the soil ecosystem requires by sampling the soil and determining what is missing. The farmer will also take his time to eradicate weeds in the soil before he plants his seeds.

He understands the weeds will kill and choke out his crops before they have time to grow. He understands the importance and benefit he derives from soil and the importance of managing the soil ecosystem. It is into this soil that he plants his yearly crops.

Your life is like the soil ecosystem. You must care for and tend to your life, just as the farmer takes care of the soil, if you want to grow and develop. Your soil (life) is the amalgamation of your purpose, values, beliefs, and worldview. This is your starting point or baseline for your growth and development. It is in this soil you plant your seeds of life.

The better you understand why you are here, who you are, what you are capable of, and how you can achieve your life vision and strategy, the better prepared you are to live the journey.

The Seeds of Life

A seed, when it is planted, begins its life by growing its root system first before it begins to reach toward the heavens. Through the germination process, it establishes its root system, tunnels itself into the ground, and establishes a solid foundation for the plant. It sinks its roots deep for stability and survivability.

The root system continues to reach outward and downward to bring in enough life sustaining water and nutrients to grow and develop. Your life needs to incorporate the same process of building a solid root system for your stability and survivability. You need time to ingrain your beliefs, values, purpose, vision, and strategy for your life into the very core of your life.

You need time to understand who you are, what your purpose is, and how to achieve it. You need to take the time to weed out those things that will inhibit your growth, and you need to establish a path in life to grow and develop. Your root system will allow you to weather any storm, trial, and challenge if it is deeply rooted in your core beliefs, values, and worldview. When you take the time to let your roots sink deep and anchor themselves to your life, you are unstoppable.

Next, after the roots have developed and are sustaining the plant, the shoot tip of the plant breaks through the soil and begins to grow and develop.

The shoot tip grows upward to increase the height of the plant and brings in the sun's life-giving rays to create the necessary photosynthesis. This growth and development process allows the plant to begin to reach toward the sky and reach its full potential and full life. Once again, your life needs to incorporate the same growth process.

With a solid foundation established by your root system, you can begin to grow and develop your eight disciplines of personal development into your life so you are deeply rooted in your character, competencies, talents, skills, and abilities. This will establish a firm foundation to ensure your skills are well developed. As you grow and learn new skills and talents, your base provides you with the experience and knowledge to make decisions.

Through your experiences of success and failure, you learn valuable lessons that you can use as a leader of your life and in life. As you continue to reach your full potential, you continue to seek out opportunities for growth and development and opportunities to use your skills to sharpen your capability.

Finally, the plant also grows outward to increase the diameter at the base of the plant. This ensures, with the root system, the base of the plant grows to support the growth of the plant. The plant diameter grows to support the upward growth of the plant and to allow it to bend but not break under the stresses of the environment.

You need to continually, grow, develop, and reinvent yourself so you have a solid foundation in the eight disciplines of personal growth to ensure you are well rooted in your skills. The signs of growth and development are present in your life and you reap your harvest.

The Harvest

The farmer has meticulously tended and cared for the crops as they have grown and matured. He is ready to harvest the crop. However, despite his best efforts, weeds and other unwanted plants have grown up, too. The weeds and unwanted plants may cause harm to the good crop, but the farmer will not eradicate the weeds until harvest time to avoid harming the overall crop. He is patient and waits until the time of reaping to eliminate the weeds.

There are three components of harvesting. The first component is reaping or the cutting of the grain, wheat, or fruit from the ground or vine. This is where the weeds and crops are reaped together. The weeds will then be gathered and destroyed. The good crops continue with the harvesting process.

After the reaping comes the threshing component, or the breaking of the hardened shell or chaff from the grain inside. This separates the covering so the true grain, the good stuff, is evident. After threshing comes the winnowing component.

Winnowing separates the chaff from the wheat. The good grain, which is good for bread and cereal, is separated. This leaves only the good grain. Everything else left over is destroyed.

You are the Farmer

The first thing you need to do on your journey is to discover your true self. You need to discover the authentic you. Life is not about an individual achievement, experience, or person. The most important undertaking of your life is not what you do, but whom you can and will become.

Unstoppable Life Matrix

The Unstoppable Life Matrix describes four quadrants of living a purposeful and unstoppable life. The vertical axis measures your personal insight and self-awareness. The horizontal axis measures the degree of personal mastery or self-control you have in your life.

Unstoppable Life Matrix

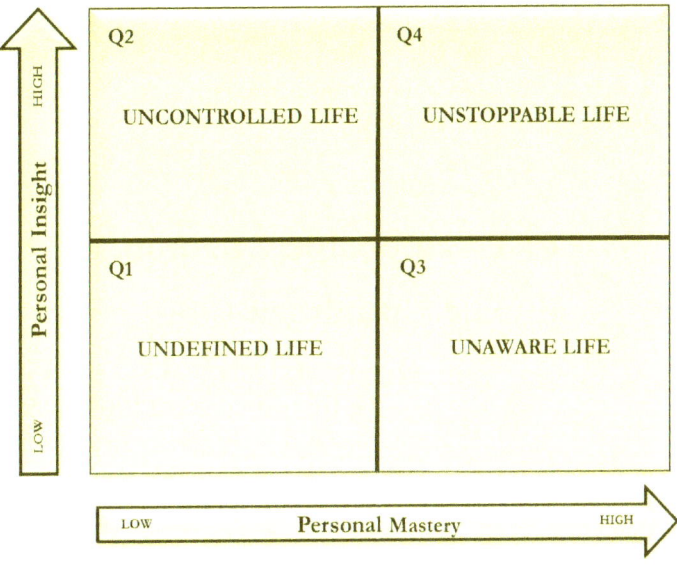

As you move along the four quadrants of the Life Matrix, you move from being lost in life to surviving to a thriving and Unstoppable Life. This life is realized through the triad of transformational growth of continuous growth, continuous development, and constantly reinventing yourself.

Quadrant 1 (Low PI/Low PM) this is the Undefined Life quadrant and characterized by uncertainty and ambiguity

Quadrant 2 (High PI/Low PM) this is the Uncontrolled Life quadrant and characterized by strong self-awareness and lack of self-control

Quadrant 3 (Low PI/High PM) this is the Unaware Life quadrant and characterized by strong self-control coupled with lack of personal insight or incomplete understanding of their full capability.

Quadrant 4 (High PI/High PM) this is the Unstoppable Life quadrant and characterized by a strong self-mastery and strong personal insight.

The Unstoppable Quadrants
The Undefined Life

Quadrant 1 (Low PI/Low PM) this is the Undefined Life quadrant and characterized by uncertainty and ambiguity. This is a person with low personal mastery coupled with a low degree of personal insight or awareness.

This is a person living an uninspired, indecisive, and directionless life. Life without direction is useless. This person lacks a personal vision for their life, has no established personal goals, and lacks a disciplined approach to living life.

The Uncontrolled Life

Quadrant 2 (High PI/Low PM) this is the Uncontrolled Life quadrant and characterized by strong self-awareness and lack of self-control. This is a person with a high degree of personal insight and self-awareness but a low degree of self-control and personal mastery.

This person understands who they are and understands their purpose in life but lacks the self-mastery to live an unstoppable life. They do not have a disciplined approach to life development, lack control of their life, and allow outside influences to control their outcomes.

The Unaware Life

Quadrant 3 (Low PI/High PM) this is the Unaware Life quadrant and characterized by strong self-control coupled with lack of personal insight or incomplete understanding of their full capability.

This is a person with a high degree of self-control and personal mastery coupled with a low degree of personal insight or self-awareness. This person understands their capabilities and abilities but lacks a personal vision, purpose, and character development. They do not have a disciplined approach to self-discovery and reflection.

The Unstoppable Life

Quadrant 4 (High PI/High PM) this is the Unstoppable Life quadrant and characterized by a strong self-mastery and strong personal insight. This person has a disciplined approach to living life.

This is a person with a high degree of self-control and personal mastery coupled with a high degree of personal insight or self-awareness. This person understands their capabilities and abilities and has a well-defined personal vision, purpose, and character development. They have a disciplined approach to self-discovery and reflection.

> **This person is living the Unstoppable Life!**

Living in Quadrant 4

Anything is possible when you choose to believe in yourself, your life's purpose, and your talents, skills, and abilities. Your life purpose unleashes you to live your life and allows you to be unstoppable. Your greatest power in life is the liberty to choose. It is

the liberty to choose what you want to do with your life, where you want to go, and what you want to become.

No one can take this power away from you; it is yours alone. You can do what you want to do; you can be who you want to be. You can live an empowered life through your decisions and choices each day. Your choices determine your attitude and your altitude. When you follow a strong and empowering purpose, you will be Unstoppable.

You cannot control every aspect of your life; you can, however, prepare yourself to be flexible and adaptive in how you react to your unexpected life and leadership challenges. Since you cannot control an environment that is volatile, uncertain, complex, and ambiguous, you can prepare yourself for the uncertainty through a disciplined approach of growth and development.

A disciplined approach also allows you to prioritize and categorize your goals so you can target which goals will provide you the most benefit first. When you begin a development plan, you need the right mindset and a "must change" attitude in order to shape and mold your talent. You must want to change and reinvent yourself.

Develop and Grow Yourself

One of the best lessons I learned early in my career was to have a plan for lifelong learning in order to develop and grow myself. If I wanted the opportunity to be a good leader and a good supervisor, I needed to improve myself. Your success is a by-product of lifelong learning. To be unstoppable you need to understand who you are and how you operate as a human being first before you can lead others. This is self-leadership.

Self-leadership requires a commitment to lifelong learning. A leader knows and understands their strengths, weaknesses, capabilities, abilities, and their emotions. Not only are education and learning an individual imperative, I believe they are the key to life's success. In order to get ahead in your work, in your life, or as a leader, you need to commit to deliberate and continuous learning each day of your life. Growth ensures that your life is not static and you will expand your life's boundaries.

This is an indispensable element of self-leadership. As a leader, you need to ask yourself: What do I need to learn today to be a better leader? What leadership skills or management techniques will help me be more effective? What are my blind spots that I need to fix? Continuous learning and continuous development creates the self-knowledge for a leader to continually reinvent their capability as a leader and a person. You need a clear picture of who you are and what you can become.

Self-awareness provides you the awareness of the gaps in your life that you need to fix in order to move from the "as-is" to the to-be." You need to recognize your areas of improvement and the development gaps that are created in your life. In addition, until you take the time to understand your strengths, weaknesses, capabilities, abilities, and your emotions, the gaps between the "as-is" and the "to-be" widens. You cannot control the span of your life—but you can control its breadth and depth.

Triad of Transformational Growth

Continuous Development

The first way you improve your C4 is through Continuous Development or CD. You must continually develop your eight disciplines of development to stay on the leading edge and moving forward in life. This type of development hones your life competencies and builds resiliency into your life.

Continuous Growth

The second way is through Continuous Growth or CG. Coupled with your continuous development of your internal and external capabilities and abilities is the continuous growth process. Growth is your self-discipline and self-commitment to apply and incorporate the lessons learned during your development to your character and leadership abilities. Without growth, you will never become the leader you want to be or need to be.

Continuously Reinventing Yourself

Finally, the last part of the model is CR, which stands for Continuously Reinventing Yourself. As you grow and develop your character, competence, leadership abilities, and your capabilities, you will continually reinvent or rebrand who you are and what you are capable of accomplishing.

Everything in your personal change management (Continuously Reinventing Yourself) is driven by a change in your vision, values, mission, experiences, and the need for you to align your goals and effects to achieve your desired outcomes. A good way to remember this: as you grow and develop, you are expanding your mind and changing your life.

Continuous Change

Your growth and development are not a "one-time fill the square" event. They are constant and persistent. The principles of continuous growth, development, experience, and reinventing yourself are found in continuous change.

The Continuous Change process is a constant reminder that learning is a lifelong process and necessary to be a better leader every day.

To keep pace with the ever-increasing demand of knowledge and pace of change in the world, you need to deliberately improve your personal and leadership ability.

Creating a life strategy or game plan will require you to reinvent yourself as you grow and develop. Reinventing yourself is the same process a Phoenix, the legendary bird that rises from the ashes to begin life anew, takes each time it goes through transformation.

To achieve something that you have never achieved before, you must reinvent yourself first. You must grow and develop qualities, skills, talents, and characteristics that you do not have today. You must learn to be flexible and adaptive to become that new person.

To become truly successful in reinventing yourself, you need to clarify where you want to go, establish a plan, write it down, and believe it in your heart, mind, body, and soul.

The Enduring Learning Model

The way to bridge that gap between your "as-is" and "to-be" is the Enduring Learning Model. It is a constant reminder that learning is a lifelong process and is necessary to become better every day. You need to keep stretching and growing yourself each day and constantly seeking ways to improve your life and career skills.

Each day is an opportunity to learn and grow your mind and achieve your potential. The Enduring Learning Model is a deliberate and targeted approach to focus your learning and development.

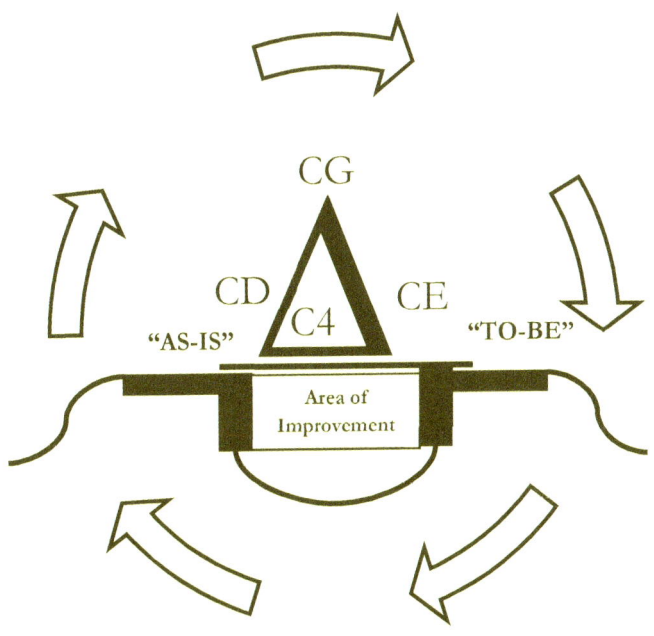

The model demonstrates that learning is not a one-time event, but a continuous process of continuous development (CD), continuous growth (CG), and continuous experiences (CE) that you internalize to shape your Character, Competence, Courage, and Commitment (C4).

- Δ – The Greek symbol DELTA represents change or difference. Change as a leader is a constant. The changes you make daily and throughout your life will make a difference in your leadership and your life.

- C4 – Character, Competence, Courage, and Commitment – C4 is the most explosive part of the function of (x) because it represents who you are deep down inside, your abilities, your strengths, and your passion.

- CD – Continuous Development – As a leader you must continually develop yourself professionally, technically, mentally, spiritually, and physically to stay on the leading edge and to be the example for others to follow.

- CG – Continuous Growth – Growth is the discipline and commitment to apply and incorporate the learned development to your character and leadership abilities.

- CE – Continuous Experience – The lifelong model adds your life and leadership experiences to the continuum. Experience is the lesson we learn as a leader that we need to apply to our growth and development.

In addition, continuous learning provides a leader the necessary knowledge to stay current on today's trends, but also flexible and adaptive to face tomorrow's challenges.

Deliberate Learning

As an adjunct professor at Bellevue University, I have the great privilege of teaching students and watching them grow and develop. The course I teach is the Kirkpatrick Signature Series, which focuses on American vision and values, your responsibility as a citizen of America, and the complexities we have as a Nation. It's a course that stretches the students' values and beliefs.

Each student starts the course with his or her opinion of what America stands for and what the problems are in our Country. Over a 12-week course of open discussion, readings, writing assignments, and a civic project, many of the students' opinions change as they open the aperture of their mind and allow their personal biases to drop.

They have learned to get out of their comfort zones and grow and challenge themselves. They have increased the knowledge of how others view America and they have shared their opinions objectively and freely. It is a key part of the course.

Today, knowledge and wisdom are key parts of achieving success. Success comes to those who have the best information, can effectively communicate ideas, and can use the knowledge to make an impact on others. Knowledge is power and valuable.

Therefore, deliberate learning is your key to the future. Deliberate learning is an investment in your future and your success. The more you know, the more you grow. The more you learn, the more you earn.

- Deliberate learning allows you to identify your strengths and weaknesses to improve your leadership effectiveness.

- Deliberate learning helps you become more self-aware and improves your leadership capability.

- Deliberate learning increases your potential in your personal life, your organization, and with your people.

- Deliberate learning helps you to improve your decision-making and thinking skills in your life and leadership.

- Deliberate learning helps you be more flexible and adaptive in your personal and professional life.

- Deliberate learning keeps you in the driver's seat and keeps you more in control of your future.

- Deliberate learning helps you stay competitive by developing new capabilities and skills.

- Deliberate learning increases your capability for critical thinking and logical analysis.

- Deliberate learning provides an opportunity to take responsibility for your life, actions, behaviors, and decisions.

- Deliberate learning allows you to take risks and move beyond your secure comfort zone.

Pathways to Developing Yourself

Read

Become a reading sponge and soak in knowledge. Read books, articles, and critical reviews in your technical expertise to improve and develop your professional competence.

At the same time, read books and articles concerning leadership and self-development to build and grow yourself and your leadership competency. Never stop reading, it helps to expand your mind.

Educational Opportunities

Seek out educational opportunities to grow yourself. Use college and continuing education courses to grow and develop your critical thinking skills and your knowledge. Attend workshops and seminars to stay current on up-to-date information concerning your career and leadership. Use workshops and seminars to fill in gaps in your learning.

Experience, Personality, and Leadership Assessments

An important part of the developmental process is leadership and life experiences. Experience is a valuable teacher and a necessary part of leadership growth. A major challenge early in your career can shape how you react and deal with future leadership challenges.

Throughout my years of leadership I have had the opportunity to use assessment tools to help find out more about who I was as a leader. I used three 360-Degree multi-rater assessments and eleven other assessment instruments to help me further my leadership capability.

Summary

You reap what you sow. Be a lifelong learner who is agile, adaptive and reflective, who learns from experiences, training, development, and successes and failures. You need to continuously develop, grow, and reinvent yourself through continuous learning, and development. You need to develop your talents, skills, capabilities, and leadership potential. You need to be refining your abilities daily.

Live Life Deliberately!

REFLECTION TIME

Give yourself some quiet time—20 minutes to start and reflect on who you truly are.

Personal Self-Assessment

Review the statements and select the answer that best fits how you assess your life at this moment.

I continue to grow and develop myself.

    1 2 3 4 5 6 7 8 9 10

I seek opportunities to challenge and grow myself.

    1 2 3 4 5 6 7 8 9 10

I choose to live my life stretching my comfort zones.

    1 2 3 4 5 6 7 8 9 10

I am alive, awake, and ready to make change in my life.

    1 2 3 4 5 6 7 8 9 10

My life is not static but constantly improving and changing.

    1 2 3 4 5 6 7 8 9 10

My challenges help to define and refine me.

    1 2 3 4 5 6 7 8 9 10

I refuse to live in my comfort zones.

    1 2 3 4 5 6 7 8 9 10

I use deliberate learning to improve and develop my life.

    1 2 3 4 5 6 7 8 9 10

I will persevere and persist to become Unstoppable.

    1 2 3 4 5 6 7 8 9 10

Self-Assessment Analysis

10-39 Points – You need to increase your self-awareness and self-efficacy. Take the time to do a deep dive on yourself to find out who you are and how to improve your life. If you want your life to be a masterpiece, you need to be the master of the pieces of your life.

40-70 Points – You have a good understanding of who you are but have areas that you need to grow and develop. Which area of your life do you need to improve? What effects do you need to implement to produce better outcomes?

71-89 Points – You are well on your way to being unstoppable in your life. You are living an abundant life and you understand the Principle of the Harvest. You know your true self and you are living your true purpose. Keep your eye on the prize and keep pressing forward.

90-100 Points – You are unstoppable. You are the Master of the Pieces of your life. However, do not stop now. You need to continue to grow, develop, and continually reinvent yourself.

UNSTOPPABLE TAKEAWAYS
Grow and Develop

You are responsible for your growth and development. Endeavor to become a lifelong learner in all aspects of your life. Apply self-leadership practices to create the outcomes you desire. Understand who you are and what you can accomplish.

Lead Yourself Well

Self-leadership is the key to leading yourself well and then leading others. Be the leader you want to be by developing yourself first. Dedicate yourself to lifelong learning. Keep your mind open to new ways of thinking.

ARE YOU BREATHING A.I.R?

Take a moment to reflect on your life. Look at the chart of actions, impacts, and results and use it as a road map to guide you on your Journey. What is your next step in your expedition?

ACTIONS	**IMPACT**
• Develop Yourself • Sink your roots deep • Stretch Yourself • Get moving • Deliberately learn	• A Life of Growth • Discover your blind spots • Ready for opportunity

RESULTS
• Living outside your comfort zone • A life of possibilities

CHAPTER 8

A DISCIPLINED MIND

"With good judgment, little else matters. Without it, nothing else matters."
Noel Tichy

"Enthusiasm is one of the most powerful engines of success. When you do a thing, do it with all your might. Put your whole soul into it. Stamp it with your own personality. Be active, be energetic, be enthusiastic and faithful, and you will accomplish your objective. Nothing great was ever achieved without enthusiasm."
Ralph Waldo Emerson

Thirty-Six Hours

"The future is always decided by those who put their imagination to work, who challenge the unknown, and who are not afraid to risk failure."
General Bernard A. Shriever

I remember the day vividly when Colonel Curlett knocked on my door, said one of our convoys had been hit, and we had casualties. I was awake immediately and at the same time had a sick feeling in my gut. In a matter of moments, we were in the car heading to the battle staff for more information and to fully understand the gravity of the situation.

Upon arriving we learned that the lead vehicle had been struck by an Improvised Explosive Device and that we had two casualties, but we did not know how bad. For two very tense hours, we received information on the convoy attack and information on the rest of the Airmen assigned to the convoy.

The room was silent when Colonel Curlett informed the battle staff that A1C Eric M. Barnes had been killed in the attack. This was our first fatality in the wing since we arrived. Immediately after the announcement, the wing chaplain asked us to each take a moment and pray for his family.

I knew that our wing would get the Special Air Mission to fly the body of A1C Barnes out of Iraq and back to our wing and then home, so I asked to be manifested to fly on the mission. I felt that it was my duty, on behalf of the enlisted force, to fly to Baghdad to bring our Fallen Airman home.

Prior to leaving, at the crew briefing, we were informed that in addition to carrying A1C Barnes home, we would be carrying home eight Soldiers who also had been killed.

Twelve hours after receiving news of the convoy attack we lifted off from the airfield and headed toward Baghdad International Airport. The aircrew on that flight was eerily quiet as we headed to Baghdad. This was their largest transfer of human souls they had flown.

Upon arriving at Baghdad, the back of the C-130 was configured for the Patriot Transfer. I had been on two other Patriot Transfers before this one, but this one was different. There were nine sons going home for the last time and one of them was my Airman.

The Soldiers we carried home that night were part of several units assigned to Baghdad for the surge, so the flight line was full of the Soldiers sending off their friends. It was an emotional scene as we stood in two rows along the backside of the C-130 and rendered salutes for each of the nine flag-draped caskets that entered the plane.

After the caskets were emplaced in the plane, the Chaplain asked everyone to come aboard and then he said a prayer for each warrior at rest. After the prayer, several Soldiers said their final goodbyes, they slowly left the plane, and headed back to their units.

Twenty-four hours after receiving the news we were flying out of Baghdad and on our way back home. It was a somber and quiet flight home.

The plane was met by the Airmen of A1C Barnes' Medium Truck Detachment and another dignified formation that was conducted for each of the nine flag-draped caskets. The thirty-six hours of that day and night made a lasting impact on me. With those images still vividly embossed in my mind, I have changed.

A Changed Mind

My youngest son Jacob has commented a few times that I "changed" after I came back from my yearlong deployment. He is right, I had changed. Anyone who has been in combat or has seen the effects of combat comes back changed.

I appreciate life more, I appreciate freedom more, I appreciate family more, and I appreciate my faith more. I also find myself more aware of my surroundings, more alert to my intuition about people and situations, and I find myself more determined to live life every day.

After a year of seeing the effects of war, I have also found myself less tolerant with people who waste their lives on things that do not matter. I am less tolerant with people that do not understand what it means to "be alive" in life and they pursue things that are fleeting.

However, I have found that I have a greater passion for living with purpose and "on purpose." The key to changing your life is a deliberate process of continual growth, development, and reinventing yourself.

When you take responsibility for your life and start to lead yourself daily, you increase your self-efficacy, you boost your self-esteem, you increase your self-confidence, and you hone your self-awareness.

By taking responsibility for your life and its outcomes, you achieve success and victory for yourself. This is your life – capitalize on it – begin working with the power of your mind to create the life you really want.

The Power of C3

The power of C3 (Cognitive Command and Control) is the most important single quality of the F(X) and Unstoppable process. The Power of C3 is the power of a disciplined mind. C3 is about building the self-discipline you need to achieve your goals and dreams and the power to overcome the setbacks and challenges that will arise.

Your mind is your greatest tool to move you in an innovative, positive, and forward direction. A disciplined mind helps you to step out of your comfort zone and expand your possibilities and opportunities.

C3 is a way of starting your self-development journey. Developing and focusing your mind to achieve your desired outcomes is a key factor in life.

There is a battle that rages in your mind on a daily basis. It is a battle of positive versus negative thinking. These two opposing forces control your outlook on life. Your mind is a wonderful creation and it can achieve great and wonderful things, but in order to do so you need to defeat the negative forces.

You can repel negative thoughts and emotions by developing and employing positive emotions and thoughts on a daily basis. Positive thoughts and emotions are more powerful than negative thoughts and emotions. Positive thoughts and emotions are life-affirming.

Will you always be able to stop negativity in your life? No; however, you can make the conscious choice to change your thoughts and emotions by understanding your mind and its state.

Your life will have positive and negative phases. Whenever you start to hear negative self-talk, think positively. Focus on positive outcomes and positive thoughts. Your success is a battle between your negative and positive self.

Emotional Intelligence

Emotional intelligence is a key part of the Power of C3 and begins with getting in touch with your inner voice. It is a journey of self-awareness and self-discovery. When you are mindful of your inner voice, you make better decisions and choices.

Emotional intelligence helps you keep your mind focused by keeping your emotional state in check. Stress, emotions, and moods are key reasons why emotional intelligence is part of a disciplined mind. You are susceptible to your emotional state and moods in life. Understanding how to manage your emotions and moods can make you a better person.

According to Daniel Goleman in his book *Emotional Intelligence*, self-awareness, self-management, social awareness, and relationship management are vital assets for a leader. An emotionally intelligent leader understands that emotions can help or hinder their leadership abilities.

By learning to focus on how your emotional state affects you, you can learn to handle your emotions so they do not interfere with your desired outcomes.

The ability to manage emotions effectively is a key part of emotional intelligence and having a disciplined mind. When you learn how to manage your emotions and respond to life's challenges appropriately, you will be able to focus on the task and achieve your goals.

The P4R Mind

"Our goals can only be reached through the vehicle of a plan, in which we must fervently believe, and upon which we must vigorously act. There is no other route to success."
Pablo Picasso

You must make your mind up from the very beginning of the journey to plan and prepare for the journey. Know where you want to go, plan, and chart out the journey. The road to building yourself is demanding, so prepare yourself mentally, physically, spiritually, and emotionally for the journey. Four parts of the 6P process reside in the P4R mind.

Persistence and perseverance are the willingness to keep pressing toward your goals and outcomes despite life's challenges. P4R is the ability within yourself to weather any storm that you will face in life. Finally, the last part of P4R is being resilient and flexible to improvise, adapt, and overcome adversity.

Planning

A journey to greatness begins with a single step. Planning is the process of developing actions or plans to attain your desired goals or outcomes for your life or leadership. When making your plans, consider what you truly want to accomplish and what effects are needed to achieve your outcome.

Planning every detail of your journey is important and helps you reduce some of life's uncertainty. Planning also helps reduce personal anxiety and increases the probability that you will achieve the goals that you have set for yourself.

Preparation

Preparation is the key to a successful life and is the trademark of successful people worldwide. The more time you prepare yourself, the better equipped you are for the struggles of life.

Preparation is the process of equipping and focusing yourself on achieving your plan. You must have the right mindset and focus to carry out your plan successfully.

Roman philosopher Seneca said, "Luck is what happens when preparation meets opportunity." Make yourself lucky by being prepared. There is no such idea of being over prepared, but there are consequences of being under prepared.

Persistence

The objective of persistence is to achieve goals or outcomes in your life. Persistence allows you to keep working at your goals or outcomes until you reach the desired outcome. It is pressing on toward the goal despite all odds. Persistence permits you to attain victory when others have long abandoned the journey. Perhaps the greatest display of self-discipline is persisting when the going gets tough.

Persistence is self-discipline in action. Persistence is the great measure of individual human character. Your persistence is, in fact, the true measure of your belief in yourself and your ability to succeed. Each time you persist in the face of adversity and disappointment, you build the habit of persistence.

You build pride, power, and self-esteem into your character and your personality. You become stronger and more resolute. By persisting, you become more self-disciplined. You develop within yourself the iron quality of success, the one quality that will carry you forward and over any obstacle that life can throw in your path.

Just as a professional athlete prepares for winning a gold medal, you need to prepare yourself for life's opportunities. All great men and women have had to endure tremendous trials and tribulations before reaching the heights of success and achievement. The strength of character manifested in their unshakable resolve made them great.

Perseverance

Perseverance is to endure a difficult situation with resolute determination and to stay in a situation even when you would rather give up. John Quincy Adams said, "Courage and perseverance have a magical talisman, before which difficulties disappear and obstacles vanish into air." Perseverance requires your entire emotional, physical, and spiritual forte to tolerate or overcome the situation. By persevering and not giving in you gain strength in your life and leadership.

Resilience

Resiliency is keeping strong emotionally, physically, mentally, and spiritually to be fit, healthy, positive, and prepared for all life's challenges. When you have a firm understanding of your life's purpose, you are more resilient to adversity. You cannot predict the future, but you can prepare for it by being resilient.

Ensure that you have life contingencies built into your plan so that you can fall back in your progress toward your goals. Know where you want to go, then plan and chart out the journey.

The road to building yourself is demanding, so prepare yourself mentally, physically, spiritually, and emotionally for the journey.

Green Bay Packers Coach Vince Lombardi said that success is being your very best. "The price of success is hard work, dedication to the job at hand, and the determination that whether we win or lose, we have applied the best of ourselves to the task at hand." The Power of P4R is summed up in the Rudyard Kipling poem:

"IF"

If you can keep your head when all about you
    Are losing theirs and blaming it on you,
If you can trust yourself when all men doubt you,
    But make allowance for their doubting too;
If you can wait and not be tired by waiting,
    Or being lied about, don't deal in lies,
Or being hated, don't give way to hating,
    And yet don't look too good, nor talk too wise:

If you can dream—and not make dreams your master;
    If you can think—and not make thoughts your aim;
If you can meet with Triumph and Disaster
    And treat those two impostors just the same;
If you can bear to hear the truth you've spoken
    Twisted by knaves to make a trap for fools,
Or watch the things you gave your life to, broken,
    And stoop and build 'em up with worn-out tools:

If you can make one heap of all your winnings
    And risk it on one turn of pitch-and-toss,
And lose, and start again at your beginnings
    And never breathe a word about your loss;

If you can force your heart and nerve and sinew
    To serve your turn long after they are gone,
And so hold on when there is nothing in you
    Except the Will which says to them: "Hold on!"

If you can talk with crowds and keep your virtue,
    Or walk with Kings—nor lose the common touch,
If neither foes nor loving friends can hurt you,
    If all men count with you, but none too much;
If you can fill the unforgiving minute
    With sixty seconds' worth of distance run,
Yours is the Earth and everything that's in it,
    And—which is more—you'll be a Man, my son!

The Positive Mind

"The pessimist complains about the wind. The optimist expects it to change. The leader adjusts the sails."
William Arthur Ward

The Positive Mind is a proactive approach to your life. Positive thinking means you approach life's challenges with a positive outlook and mindset. It does not mean you avoid or ignore the bad things that happen in your life or the difficult challenges you will face; instead, you make it through by perseverance and persistence.

Do you know that you are more powerful than you think? You have tremendous power as an individual and by applying this power you can be unstoppable and you can have the life you want.

The true power of the Positive Mind is more than positive thinking or a positive attitude, it is a way of life. It is a continuous state of mind. It is a mindset that no matter what life challenges you with, the good and the bad, you keep your life on the positive aspects of life and a positive belief in yourself and your abilities. You will handle life differently if you shape your focus toward the positive versus allowing yourself to focus on the negative.

A positive outlook will tell you that there is a light at the end of every tunnel and it is called Hope. Hope gives you the determination and willpower to overcome the challenges. A negative outlook would convince you that the light at the end of the tunnel is a train heading your way.

The Power of the Positive is changing the voice in your head from the negative to the positive. When you focus on expanding your positive self-talk, you expand your ability to produce positive outcomes and positive self-esteem. By focusing on the positives in your life you create an optimistic outlook in your life and begin to see a life full of possibilities.

The Positive Mindset

What is your outlook on life? Do you tend to see the water glass as half-empty or half full? How you view the glass relates directly to your positive or negative outlook on life. A positive mindset plays an important role in a positive outlook on life. Research has found that positive thinking can build resilience in your life, help in your daily stress management, and help in your overall physical and mental well-being.

Remember: You cannot change what happens to you, but you can always choose how you respond. A positive mindset is viewing yourself, your purpose, your talents, and your capabilities in a positive way. It is a mindset of optimism.

When you look at life as abundance versus scarcity, you begin to see the possible versus the impossible. A positive mindset is a proactive approach to directing your thoughts and feelings about your life. It is a way of ridding yourself of the negativity of life.

Let me back track one step. You will have trials and tribulations in your life. You will experience setbacks and failures. However, how you approach those events is up to you. Your reactions and responses are outcomes you can direct.

Part of the F(X) Model is the effects you need to put in your life to change or direct the outcomes. It is also a way of asking the "what ifs" of your life and preparing yourself now for the "what ifs" of the future.

You can create a positive mindset for the trials and tribulations. It is too easy to focus on the negative. When you focus on the negative, you allow your stressed mind and tired body to think negative thoughts and seek solace in self-pity.

A positive mindset can help you overcome feelings of negativity and self-despair. A positive mindset helps you strengthen your self-confidence and improve your self-confidence. Here are some ways to establish your mindset.

- **Let go of the past and strive toward the future.** Your past does not equal the future. Past trials and tribulations do not define your future, but they can help you to define a brighter future. Use your past negative experiences to shape your character and shape your future decisions.

- **Bad things happen and will happen…press on anyway.** Your personal value and self-worth come from deep inside you and are not dictated by outside circumstances. You do not have to be a victim of your circumstances. Life has a way of conveying change to your life. Focus on the Power of the Positives and press on through the bad.

- **Put effects into place to create your desired outcomes.** Stop your negative thoughts about what has happened to you and begin your positive thinking about what you can make happen. Life involves risk-taking every day, take the risk and make your positive life happen--set positive goals and take action!

- **Life is too short to live it negatively.** Remind yourself every day that life is too short to be a pessimist. Make every minute of your life count by being proactive and focus yourself on what life has to offer.

- **Be focused on good.** Be a rational optimist who takes the good with the bad in hopes of the good ultimately outweighing the bad, and with the understanding that being pessimistic about everything accomplishes nothing. Prepare for the worst but hope for the best--the former makes you sensible, and the latter makes you an optimist.

- **Focus and analyze your thoughts.** When you encounter a challenging situation, try to notice how you think about what is happening. Do you engage in negative self-talk? Do you mentally criticize yourself or others? This negative thinking presents a major obstacle, but identifying such thoughts is the first step in overcoming them.

- **Be thankful for the good things in life.** Celebrate and focus on the positive aspects of your life--family, friends, achievements, and capabilities. Your positive thoughts will help to push the inconsequential negative thoughts out of your life. Think about the good things in your life every day.

- **Focus on your self-talk.** What do you think or say when a setback or challenge comes your way? Do you positively or negatively self-talk? You need to concentrate on your self-talk and harness your inner monster. Watch carefully for negative self-limiting self-talk.

Optimism
Be transformed by the renewing of your mind.
Romans 12:2

Optimism is a powerful motivator and a part of the Power of the Positive. Optimism is a positive approach to life. It is looking at life and expecting the best outcome to happen no matter what circumstances life hands you. Being optimistic is being positive and being your own agent of hope.

Being optimistic means you are not afraid to seek out life's opportunities. You see the positive aspects of life versus the negative. Looking at life in an optimistic way provides you the confidence and courage to tackle life head on.

Optimism begins in your mind and changes your attitude toward life. Optimism is not a life of fantasy, but an acceptance of the realities of life. Being optimistic is hard work. Optimism requires that you build your persistence and perseverance to endure the negativity of a situation. Being optimistic allows you to focus yourself on positive outcomes while chaos surrounds. This is not an easy task and a positive outcome of optimism is personal resilience.

Finally, to utilize an optimistic lifestyle to its fullest, you need to ingrain it as a permanent part of your life.

Traits of Optimism

- Creates a positive atmosphere for yourself
- Fosters a climate of innovations and creativity
- Communicates a positive lifestyle
- Views setbacks as opportunity for learning
- Looks for opportunity hidden in situations
- Does not get discouraged easily

Optimism is contagious…catch it!

A Warrior-Focused Mind

One way we develop young men and women to prepare for combat is to prepare their bodies and their minds. One area we focus on developing is a Warrior-Focused Mind in each individual. Having a Warrior-Focused Mind is understanding the world around you with clarity and focus.

It is a mindset of preparedness and understanding of the uncertainty and complexity of your environment. The world has changed; it is a volatile, uncertain, complex, and ambiguous (VUCA) environment, which means you need to prepare yourself to manage current and future challenges and opportunities.

What do I mean by VUCA?

> ➤ **Volatile** means that the speed, size, and scale of change in the world today has a great impact on events around the globe almost instantaneously. An example is the rate and pace of stock market changes and the effect it has on personal and corporate wealth.
>
> ➤ **Uncertainty** means that world events are unpredictable and this unpredictability makes it impossible to prepare for unknown world events. An example is the effects of Arab Spring and governmental changes in the last four years.
>
> ➤ **Complexity** means that the chaotic nature of the world combined with the volatility and uncertainty of global events creates an environment of confusion and difficulty for today's leaders.
>
> ➤ **Ambiguity** means that there is a lack of clarity or transparency surrounding world events. It is hard to predict what threats are in the world if you do not know the who, what, or why things are happening.

Developing a Warrior-Focused Mind is a mindset of thinking critically under pressure. It is constantly thinking of options versus getting too comfortable with a predictable outcome.

It is thinking non-linear and preparing yourself for uncertainty. It is developing flexible and adaptive thinking strategies and learning to lead change quickly and responsively. A Warrior-Focused Mind means being able to critically analyze problems and situations and foresee 2nd, 3rd, and 4th order of effects and actions.

This requires thinking long term, being future-oriented, and having a mental picture or visualization of what the outcome needs to be or look like in the future.

A Warrior-Focused Mind is having the capability to act in an influential, urgent, and steadfast way to realize outcomes and results. With a Warrior-Focused Mind you understand and can operate in a volatile, uncertain, complex, and ambiguous world.

You comprehend risk and manage it to achieve desired results. Having a Warrior-Focused Mind creates the mental toughness you need to become fearless.

Thinking Tactics

The following thinking tactics can help you to think critically under pressure and to critically think through complex and uncertain problems and challenges. The thinking tactics are time-sensitive and require an understanding of how you think and operate.

Change is a constant in a VUCA environment and to remain successful and unstoppable you must be able positively respond to continuous change. You must learn to have the capability to lead through continuous change and learn to be adaptive and flexible throughout the change process.

Improvise, Adapt, and Overcome

Throughout my time in the Military I have had the pleasure of working with several United States Marine

Corps Senior Enlisted from the. Two sayings or phrases I heard several times were "Semper Fi" and "Improve, Adapt, and Overcome". Semper Fi or Semper Fidelis means "Always Faithful". A Marine is always faithful to the mission and to each other.

"Improvise, Adapt, and Overcome" which emphasize the importance of innovative thinking, flexibility, and prevailing in unexpected and uncertain situations. These three words are part of the Warrior Focused Mind process and are a way of thinking, creatively and adaptively, to develop a flexible and adaptive mindset to deal with uncertainty and ambiguity.

Improvise

Improvising is an essential thinking skill. In a VUCA environment, improvising is being able to create opportunities and solutions in an unexpected challenge or situation. It is a form of innovative and creative thinking that allows you to use whatever is at hand to overcome the situation.

If you saw the TV Show "MacGyver" then you know what I mean by using whatever is at hand to overcome the situation. The ability to improvise in uncertain and ambiguous situations allows you to think unconventionally and, with a degree of confidence, to meet the challenge and resolve the situation.

Adapt

The ability to adapt is another key life skill. Adaptability is the ability to be flexible and agile during changing and complex environments. Being able to adapt to your surroundings in order to create a brighter future is a key part of adaptability. In a VUCA environment, adaptability is being able to be flexible and adaptive to the situation and coming out stronger and more able to handle challenges.

Overcome

Overcoming is another key thinking skill which I call Victory Thinking. This is a positive mindset that you have the ability to handle and overcome any situation. In a VUCA environment, overcoming is about creating the outcomes you want in life and positively responding to the situation. It is having the confidence to attack the situation and to be able to persevere and persist until you triumph. Overcoming means you are the Victor not the Victim of the situation.

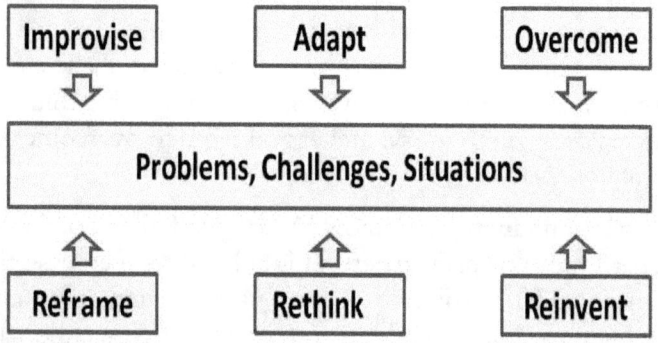

Reframe, Rethink, Reinvent

These set of thinking skills require more time and emphasize the importance of systems, strategic, and adaptive thinking. Reframing requires you to take the time to break down the complex problem into its smallest component and relook at the problem as a system of problems to develop a solution. Rethinking is taking the time to review and analyze what you did in the past to see if it will work again or to help develop a new solution to the problem. Finally, reinvent is a clean sheet thinking approach to solving your problem.

Reframe

Reframing is a deliberate and reflective way of thinking to solve complex problems. It is a process of looking at a problem, not just in one way, but also in several different or alternative ways. Reframing a problem or situation allows you to think about the "What ifs" of a problem. What if we solve it this way versus the way we always have solved it? What is the outcome if we solve it this way? Reframing takes time and require expertise in the problem you are solving but allow you to think about creating new outcomes to known problems or situations. In a VUCA environment, reframing a problem may help to reduce the complexity and ambiguity of the problem.

Rethink

Rethinking is a reflective way of thinking about problems and challenges. It is reviewing what you did in the past and why it worked. Rethinking poses several questions in the review process. Why did my last approach work? How did it work? Was the outcome the one I intended? What steps did I use in solving the problem? Did I think of alternative outcomes during my though process? Rethinking is taking the time to analyze what you did in the past and learning from the process then using this information for future decision-making.

Reinvent

Reinventing is a clean sheet approach to thinking or decision-making. The most significant outcome of clean sheet thinking is the new perspective it brings to your decision-making. By using a clean sheet approach you discard your biases, predispositions, and preconceptions.

Clean sheet thinking allows you to look at challenges and problems as if you never had seen them before. Reinventing allows you to capitalize on opportunities you may have missed during your early decision-making.

Effects Mindset

Each morning ask yourself this questions before you begin your day: How will I live my life today? How will I use today to live out my purpose? What life decisions will I make today? How will those decisions impact my future? What effects do I need to put into my life today to live an Unstoppable Life?

Why should you ask these questions? You need to understand what you are going to do so you design your life versus allowing it to happen. Abraham Lincoln said;

> There are no accidents in my philosophy. Every effect must have its cause. The past is the cause of the present, and the present will be the cause of the future. All these are links in the endless chain stretching from the finite to the infinite.

Lincoln understood the Law of Cause and Effect. If you want to live an Unstoppable Life, you must understand the Law of Cause and Effect and then create the effects you want in your life to produce the outcomes you desire. By creating the effects, you start to remove the ambiguity and uncertainty in your life.

The FORGE Process is your choice to use the space between action and choice. Viktor Frankl and Stephen Covey both explain that between stimulus and response that we have an opportunity to decide what our action will be. The space between is our greatest freedom. It is your choice to be proactive or reactive.

Ultimately, you are responsible and accountable for your success in life. Personal development and growth occurs in one of two basic ways: it happens either as an unplanned event or by deliberate planning and preparation. Your goal is to deliberately improve your life.

No matter what your intention, the FORGE Process model can be applied to help you improve, grow, and develop all aspects of your life. You are in control of your response and you are in control of the outcome.

Effects are proactive and are not reactive. Effects are an essential requirement for outcome achievement and must be congruent with your purpose, values, and beliefs. Effects are your way of achieving your desired outcome. Successfully achieving your desired outcome requires that you have the necessary skills, abilities, talents, or resources to create the effects needed.

Using effects based mindset thinking, you would ask yourself the following questions:

- What type of effects would be most appropriate in the given set of circumstances?
- What actions and decisions do you need to make in order to achieve your desired outcome?
- What internal and external skills, abilities, talents, and resources do you have that will help you to achieve the desired outcome?

- What skills, talents, abilities, and resources do you need to learn or develop to achieve the desired outcome?

The effects mindset is a focused way to change the effects in your life and to create the outcome or consequence that you desire. In every situation you face, you can choose how to respond and what to do or not to do.

Outcome Mindset Process

The first thing you need to do in the Outcome Mindset Process is to determine if the outcome is something you truly desire. Are you committed to achieving the outcome? Are you passionate about the end state?

If it is something you are willing to pursue and achieve, then the second thing you need to decide is how much energy and strength you want to exert to achieve the outcome. How driven are you to make the outcome a reality?

Are you willing to trade minutes, hours, days, or even years of your life to achieve the outcome? If you are willing to pay the price to achieve the outcome, then the third thing you need to do is create the effect(s) you need to achieve the outcome.

It is important to note that the effect(s) of a given action may set off other changes or one event may trigger subsequent outcomes. All actions have unintended consequences both good and bad.

Visualize Your Outcome What is it?	- A state of being? - A skill, talent, or capability? - A place?
Understand your outcome	- What are the consequences of achieving the outcome? - What are the 2nd, 3rd, and 4th order of effects? - Is it attainable? - What is the price you will pay for the outcome? - Solidify your outcome - Make the outcome real and concrete - Be specific - Plan to achieve your outcome - Establish your Goals to achieve the outcome - Establish your objectives - Establish your strategy
Execute your outcome action plan!	Take action to make it happen

Fearless Focus

Fearless means conquering your mind and uncertainty. Every individual harbors fear inside of him or her. It may be fear of failure, fear of not belonging, or fear of public speaking. There are many types of fears that we can attribute to why we do not achieve something or try something in our lives.

Fear is a limiting factor in your life. Fear is a generation of the mind and is a double-edge sword. To live an unstoppable life you need to acknowledge and recognize your fears.

Our fears can protect us from killing or injuring ourselves by doing something reckless or unsafe (i.e., jumping over cars with a motorcycle).

On the other hand, fear can hold you back from realizing your dreams, goals, and living your life. Fear is a ravenous monster that can control you mind and attack your courage to live fully. It will feed on your anxieties, doubts, worries, uncertainties, and suspicions until it consumes your every thought.

If you do not make it your business to overcome fear, you better believe it will try to overwhelm you. How you develop and train your mind can help you become fearless.

Fearless means that you face your fears head on despite being afraid. It means you tackle your fear one part at a time, over a period of time. Fearless means that you will not permit your fears to get the better of you, or worse, limit your life. Fearless means getting out of your comfort zones so you can become unstoppable.

Summary

Your mind is your ultimate weapon and the more focused and developed it is will help you to meet the challenges of the present and the future. Developing and focusing your mind to achieve your desired outcomes is a crucial element in your life. You mind is your key weapon to move you in an innovative, positive, and forward direction.

Live Life Intentionally!

REFLECTION TIME

Give yourself some quiet time—20 minutes to start and reflect on who you truly are.

Personal Self-Assessment

Review the statements and select the answer that best fits how you assess your life at this moment.

I use my time purposefully and intentionally.

    1 2 3 4 5 6 7 8 9 10

I am responsible for my life and its outcomes.

    1 2 3 4 5 6 7 8 9 10

My mind is focused and prepared for life's challenges.

    1 2 3 4 5 6 7 8 9 10

Planning is an important part of my daily life.

    1 2 3 4 5 6 7 8 9 10

I continue to develop a resilient mind in order to persevere and persist in life.

    1 2 3 4 5 6 7 8 9 10

I have a positive and optimistic outlook on life.

    1 2 3 4 5 6 7 8 9 10

I view setbacks as opportunities to grow and develop.

    1 2 3 4 5 6 7 8 9 10

I choose to respond in a positive manner to life.

    1 2 3 4 5 6 7 8 9 10

I have a warrior focus in my life.

    1 2 3 4 5 6 7 8 9 10

Self-Assessment Analysis

10-39 Points – You need to increase your self-awareness and self-efficacy. Take the time to do a deep dive on yourself to find out who you are and how to improve your life. If you want your life to be a masterpiece, you need to be the master of the pieces of your life.

40-70 Points – You have a good understanding of who you are but have areas that you need to grow and develop. Which area of your life do you need to improve? What effects do you need to implement to produce better outcomes?

71-89 Points – You are well on your way to being unstoppable in your life. You are living an abundant life and you understand the Principle of the Harvest. You know your true self and you are living your true purpose. Keep your eye on the prize and keep pressing forward.

90-100 Points – You are unstoppable. You are the Master of the Pieces of your life. However, do not stop now. You need to continue to grow, develop, and continually reinvent yourself.

UNSTOPPABLE TAKEAWAYs

Develop a P4R Mind

Perseverance, planning, preparation, persistence, and resilience are keys to your growth and development. P4R is the willingness and the ability to keep pressing towards your goals and outcomes despite life's challenges. P4R is the ability within yourself to weather any storm that you will face in life.

The World has Changed

Developing yourself will ensure you can survive and thrive in the future. Look holistically at the changing world and understand your environment. Understand the complexity and uncertainty so you can improvise, adapt, and overcome your challenges and opportunities.

ARE YOU BREATHING A.I.R?

Take a moment to reflect on your life. Look at the chart of actions, impacts, and results and use it as a road map to guide you in your Journey. What is your next step in your expedition?

ACTIONS	IMPACT
<ul><li>Be Disciplined</li><li>Be Optimistic</li><li>Be Fearless</li></ul>	<ul><li>Focused Intentional Mindset</li><li>Positive Outlook</li></ul>
RESULTS	
<ul><li>A Disciplined Mind!</li><li>A Warrior-Focused Mind</li></ul>	

CHAPTER 9

LIVING LIFE UNSTOPPABLE

"Between stimulus and response, there is a space. In that space is our power to choose our response. In our response lies our growth and our freedom."
Viktor E. Frankl

"Courage is resistance to fear, mastery of fear - not absence of fear."
Mark Twain

Unstoppable Attitude

"I know the price of success: dedication, hard work, and an unremitting devotion to the things you want to see happen."
Frank Lloyd Wright

Why is an unstoppable attitude important? Because it determines everything you do in your life. Your attitude controls the way you see the world and how the world sees you every day. One of the most important effects you can put into your life is to learn to control your attitude and its influence on your life, your performance, and your relationships.

I recently met a young Airman that exemplifies how attitude can change your life. The young man is a Security Forces professional whose attitude is inspiring. I first met him as I drove through the base gate one day in February. It was 5°F outside and with the wind chill, it was -8°F.

As I rolled my window down and handed him my ID he said, "Good Morning and welcome to Paradise!" If it wasn't for his upbeat attitude and smile I would have thought he was being sarcastic.

After he finished his ID check, he handed me back my ID and said, "Have a great Air Force Day!" His greeting was the same each day--same attitude and same smile.

After a few months, the young man was moved to another post and no longer a part of my day. By chance, I met him in the hallway of my building and stopped him to ask him about his gate greeting and his positive attitude. His response to my query was amazing. He said,

> My mom, who was prior military, told me that I had a choice each day to choose my attitude. I could choose

to create the sunshine and have a positive attitude or I could choose to allow storm clouds to invade my attitude and be negative. I get to choose how I begin and end my day and each day affects the next day. Therefore, each day I choose my attitude and have a positive outlook no matter where I am or what I am dealing with. I choose to create sunshine.

He chooses each day to create sunshine. Despite the bitter cold, despite his setbacks, and despite his mistakes...he chooses to bring the sunshine. His mom taught him a valuable lesson about attitude.

Your attitude is the alpha and omega of your unstoppable life. How you choose to react and act each day starts with your attitude. Attitude is an indispensable part of an unstoppable life and a positive life.

You has a choice every morning and throughout the day in how your attitude will impact your life and its environment. You can choose a positive, self-motivating, and inspiring attitude or you can choose a negative, self-defeating, and life-destructive attitude. The choice is yours.

If you want to live an unstoppable life, you must have an unstoppable attitude. Each morning you need to wake up and let the world know that you are "alive and ready to make a difference and ready to face life's challenges."

This simple act creates a positive outlook for the day and reaffirms your belief in your abilities, capabilities, and talents to face life's challenges.

Throughout the day, you need to reinforce your positive attitude with positive thinking and life-affirming thoughts. This will strengthen your positive attitude and ready you for the rest of the day.

At the end of the day you need to take the time to review how you overcame the challenges of the day and how you kept your positive focus.

The Unstoppable-Centered Life

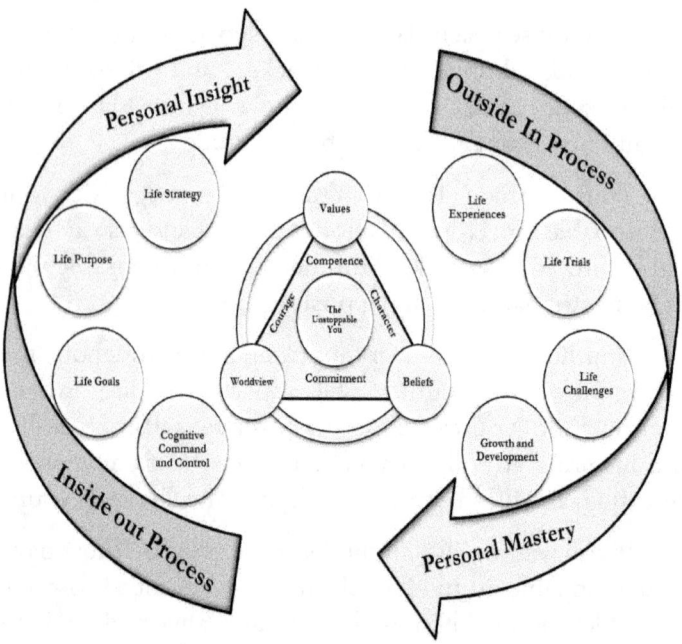

Being Unstoppable is not about becoming a superhero or suddenly receiving superpowers. You are not suddenly indestructible. Living an Unstoppable-Centered Life means you have a choice to live your life each day to its fullest. It is about you taking charge of your life, your decisions, and your actions.

It is about choosing to live congruently and integrity with your values, beliefs, and worldview despite what others may say about you. When you are living congruent to your purpose, beliefs, and values then you are living authentically. You are living out your true life when you do not compromise your true self.

Living an Unstoppable-Centered Life means you live out your true life and not the life others want you to live. Remember your time on earth is short, if you live your life in accordance with what others think or say, you will live a life unfulfilled and with regret.

Anything is possible when you choose to believe in yourself, your life's purpose, and your talents, skills, and abilities.

Your life purpose unleashes you to live your life and allows you to be unstoppable. You need to live out your purpose authentically and daily.

You need to passionately pursue your purpose in life and relentlessly challenge yourself to become better. Living an Unstoppable-Centered Life means you choose to live out your dreams, achieve your goals, and create the outcomes you want in your life. It means choosing to live out your faith, believe in yourself, and never give up on your vision of your future.

Living an Unstoppable-Centered Life means you choose to live inspired, discovering your purpose, and accepting responsibility for your life. It means you choose to continuously, grow, develop, and reinvent your life to be the very best you can be each day.

Finally, Living an Unstoppable-Centered begins with the knowledge that is up to you to create and live your unstoppable life. No one else is responsible for your life or cares about your life as much you do.

The Power Cycle

"Believe in yourself! Have faith in your abilities! Without a humble but reasonable confidence in your own powers you cannot be successful or happy."
Norman Vincent Peale

The Power Cycle are those actions or effects that you can do in your life to make it unstoppable. Each power area helps you to fulfill your purpose, vision, and mission in life and helps to increase the positives in your life.

The Power Cycle helps you to energize yourself and focus your passion on being unstoppable in life. The cycle is a way of looking at the whole of your life and ensuring you are balanced and resilient. Why is a balanced approach important in your life?

In today's chaotic, uncertain, ambiguous, and fast-paced world, you are bombarded with streams of information every day. Your mind is assaulted with the constant onslaught of emails, texts, social media, 24-hour news, work problems, community problems, and family problems.

Your heart, mind, body, and soul seldom have time to rest and reflect on your own inner information since they are in constant overload mode and stressed out. You seldom take the time to stop and recalibrate your life and see if you have gone off course.

The Power Cycle is a way of recalibrating your life and refocusing to living "on purpose." It is a reminder that although you are unstoppable, you are not indestructible.

POWER #1

Believe in Yourself

On July 31, 1981, the band Journey released their Escape album, which went multi-platinum and sold over 12 million copies worldwide. The first song on that album was the song "Don't Stop Believing." This song has become the anthem for sports teams during winning seasons, and has become the anthem for many people. The song reminds you to never stop believing, never give up, and to keep pressing on in your life. The Power of Believing is the confidence that you have in yourself to succeed.

Confidence is vital because it is the key ingredient in making a difference and an impact in your life. Confidence is your inner motivator and driver of becoming. Believing in yourself is not just a worthy thing to do, it is a personal survival skill. You need to believe in your ability to affect your life's outcomes in order to have the confidence and courage you need to meet the challenges you will face.

The Power of Believing in Yourself starts with you. You are the key to the Power of Believing. The power is entirely yours, nobody else can give you the power, and it is a manifestation of your attitude and positive mindset.

It is an unshakeable realization that your self-confidence lies inside you and is under your immediate control. Believing in yourself is an unyielding belief deep down in your core that you have the talents, gifts, skills, capabilities, and abilities to meet any challenge the world has for you. Enthusiasm, personal energy, and a positive outlook are your daily companions.

You ignite passion in others because of your self-confidence. Believing in yourself is the beginning of self-inspiration and achieving your abundant life.

You are a life lifter. You live with purpose and believe that you serve a higher purpose. You envision an inspiring future for yourself and you have a sense of connectedness with that vision. The Power of Believing is learning to master yourself first!

A Leader Who Believed in Herself

I had the honor of serving with Lieutenant General Susan Helms throughout my career, first at Air Education and Training Command, then Air Force Space Command, and finally at United States Strategic Command.

What makes Lieutenant General Helms unique? General Helms was one of the first women to attend U.S. Air Force Academy in 1980. Afterwards, NASA selected her in January 1990 to become an astronaut.

On January 13, 1993, she became the first U.S. military woman in space. She flew on STS-54 (1993), STS-64 (1994), STS-78 (1996), and STS-101 (2000), and was the first U.S. military woman to serve aboard the International Space Station as a member of the Expedition-2 crew (2001). A veteran of five space flights, General Helms has logged 211 days in space, including a spacewalk of eight hours and 56 minutes, a world record.

General Helms holds four Space records and was inducted into the NASA Astronaut Hall of Fame. She finished her service to the country as the first woman to lead the 14th Air Force "Flying Tigers" and Joint Functional Component Command for Space.

General Helms is the embodiment of the 6P Focus and the Forge Process. She took the time to grow, develop, and reinvent herself along her career. When challenges presented themselves, she took the risk and then persisted and persevered until she overcame and accomplished her goal. She is an example of an unstoppable leader!

When you fully believe in yourself you begin to recognize that you can do more than you ever thought possible. You discover new skills, new talents, and new thinking abilities that you may have never used before or even recognized. When you believe in yourself, you begin to understand what you are capable of and take the necessary risks and actions to achieve you goals.

The benefit of believing in yourself is that you begin to trust in yourself enough to risk change and unleashing your Unstoppable Life.

POWER #2
Courage and Confidence

*"Courage is doing what you're afraid to do.
There can be no courage unless you're scared."*
Eddie Rickenbacker

General William T. Sherman defines Courage as "a perfect sensibility of the measure of danger and a mental willingness to endure it." Merriam-Webster's Dictionary describes Courage as "mental or moral strength to venture, persevere, and withstand danger, fear, or difficulty." Courage is not the absence of fear, but the willingness and ability to act in the face of our fears.

Courage then demands great strength and at times great sacrifice--physically, mentally, and morally. Physical courage utilizes the strength of your body for the act of bravery. Mental courage utilizes the strength of your mind to fortify you for an act of bravery.

Moral courage means taking the moral high ground and standing up for your beliefs and values while risking alienation and ridicule by those who do not agree with you. All three are important aspects of being courageous. Physical and mental courage enables you to act in the face of danger, personal risk, or to overcome fear and complete your task or mission.

Confidence is your greatest personal resource and resilience factor. With confidence, you can face life's challenges head on and know that you will survive and thrive. Confidence is indispensable to living an unstoppable life. Confidence is an ardent belief in yourself, your capabilities, and your ability. There is nothing more powerful than your confidence. It is a life changer.

You control your confidence level. Confidence is the inner voice that steels you and lets you know you have the capability and the ability to achieve your dreams and goals. Courage is the lion's roar that says, "let's make it happen" and then charges headlong to make it happen.

First Dismounted Patrol

When I stepped out of my Humvee for my first dismounted patrol, it took a lot of physical and mental courage. Although I had trained and practiced the procedures, it was not the same as actually doing it. After opening the door and stepping out of the vehicle the reality of the situation washed over me. I was standing in the same place that an IED went off and killed A1C Elizabeth Nicole Jacobsen and Army Sergeant Steve Morin.

I was part of an eight-man team that was walking the road ahead of the vehicles to look for improvised explosive devices. Each person was assigned a section of the road up to the bridge. Each of us walked slowly looking for wires, disturbances in the dirt, and anything out of the ordinary. If you spotted something, you needed to mark the area and call for EOD to come check it out.

As we approached the bridge, two people walked the top of the bridge while I and another Airman went under the bridge and looked in the spaces under the bridge. We checked the columns and the low spaces for IEDs and landmines.

Overall, it took us 2 hours to walk 3 miles. Although the walk was uneventful on that day, the sheer act of putting myself in harm's way required physical and mental courage to make my first walk.

Moral courage gives you the strength you need to stand firm in your convictions. Moral courage allows you to do what you believe is right despite what the world around you says is right. It is also the willingness to take the negative consequences of an unpopular action. Moral courage, even if it is the right thing to do, can mean the loss of friends, reputation, and your job.

Why is moral courage important for a leader? If you lack the moral courage to hold on to your beliefs in the moment of difficulty, peer resistance, or personal opposition, then you lack confidence in yourself and lack a conviction of courage.

It takes moral courage to decide to do what is right and not necessarily what feels good. Moral courage is setting and living your standards daily and being a role model. The word parresia is a Greek word meaning to speak with great boldness and empowerment.

It means that you are confident in who you are and in your abilities and that you are courageous and unashamed of who you are. You need parresia in your life so that you are courageous like Daniel, bold like Nehemiah, and unashamed like Elijah.

The power of Courage and Confidence then, is when you display your highest quality of life. When you choose to be courageous, your hope, dignity, and inner strength grows stronger It is the moment when you are most complete and congruent with your purpose, values, beliefs, and your true self. You are meant to be courageous and live your life purposefully.

Freedom and Liberty

During my trips to the Pentagon, I would take the time to run along the National Mall in Washington D.C. and soak in American History. My running route usually started in the Constitution Gardens at the 56 Signers of the Declaration of Independence Memorial.

It was a great place to start my run through history. It reminded me of the beginning journey to Freedom and Liberty and the sacrifice each of these signers ended up making for the Founding of America.

From the Constitution Gardens I would run to the WWII Memorial, then to the D.C. War Memorial, to the Korean War Memorial, and over to the Vietnam Veteran's Memorial.

Each of the memorials along the run reminded me of the Service and the Sacrifice of the men and women, the

Sons and Daughters of America, made to found and keep the Country free. I would finish my run at the Lincoln Memorial and usually spend time reading the Gettysburg Address and Lincoln's 2nd Inaugural Address.

President Lincoln, in my opinion, showed enormous grace under pressure as a President to preserve Freedom and Liberty. He was also a great example of how to use courage, persistence, perseverance, resilience, and forgiveness as a leader and in your personal life.

First, he had courage to stand up for what he believed was right concerning the Union of the States and the U.S. Constitution. He was faced with an incredible challenge of preserving the United States when elected President.

In his first inaugural address, President Lincoln argued that the Constitution was binding to all States and could only be dissolved unanimously by all the States. He also stated that based on the Oath of the President he was solemnly bound to preserve, protect, and defend the Union of the United States.

> I am loath to close. We are not enemies, but friends. We must not be enemies. Though passion may have strained, it must not break our bonds of affection. The mystic chords of memory, stretching from every battlefield and patriot grave to every living heart and hearthstone all over this broad land, will yet swell the chorus of the Union when again touched, as surely they will be, by the better angels of our nature.

Second, President Lincoln, as he eloquently stated in his Gettysburg Address, had the persistence and perseverance to keep fighting for what he believed was right. He made sure that those who fought, bled, and died were not forgotten and the fight would continue until the Union was united once again.

Four score and seven years ago our fathers brought forth on this continent a new nation, conceived in liberty, and dedicated to the proposition that all men are created equal.

Now we are engaged in a great civil war, testing whether that nation, or any nation so conceived and so dedicated, can long endure. We are met on a great battlefield of that war. We have come to dedicate a portion of that field, as a final resting place for those who here gave their lives that that nation might live.

It is altogether fitting and proper that we should do this. But, in a larger sense, we cannot dedicate, we cannot consecrate, we cannot hallow this ground. The brave men, living and dead, who struggled here, have consecrated it, far above our poor power to add or detract. The world will little note, nor long remember what we say here, but it can never forget what they did here. It is for us the living, rather, to be dedicated here to the unfinished work which they who fought here have thus far so nobly advanced.

It is rather for us to be here dedicated to the great task remaining before us—that from these honored dead we take increased devotion to that cause for which they gave the last full measure of devotion—that we here highly resolve that these dead shall not have died in vain—that this nation, under God, shall have a new birth of freedom—and that government of the people, by the people, for the people, shall not perish from the earth.

Finally, President Lincoln displayed resilience and forgiveness after the issue was resolved. The Nation needed to move forward as one people and not enemies.

> With malice toward none, with charity for all, with firmness in the right as God gives us to see the right, let us strive on to finish the work we are in, to bind up the nation's wounds, to care for him who shall have borne the battle and for his widow and his orphan, to do all which may achieve and cherish a just and lasting peace among ourselves and with all nations.

President Lincoln displayed indispensable moral courage when he stood for Freedom and Liberty. Each of us could learn a valuable lesson when it comes to courage and forgiveness.

POWER #3
Resiliency

"Fortify thyself with contentment: that is an impregnable stronghold."
Epiticus

Serving in the Air Force for 28 years taught me the discipline of taking care of myself by being physically fit and being resilient. The Air Force instills a total fitness mindset into Airmen so they are motivated to participate in a year-round physical fitness program.

Resiliency is important because your health affects you in all eight disciplines of personal development. How do you handle crisis and tragedy in life? Do you fight back and overcome the situation or are you overwhelmed and distressed that you cannot cope? Life would be much easier if you were tough and callous to tragedy and calamity. Or would it?

You cannot escape difficulty, heartache, and suffering. As a resilient person, you will experience both negative and positive emotions during challenging situations and find positive value in the challenge. However, you can become resilient in life.

Viktor Frankl, in his book, *Man's Search for Meaning*, says that in order to be more resilient in life we must change ourselves.

> We must never forget that we may also find meaning in life even when confronted with a hopeless situation, when facing a fate that cannot be changed. For what then matters is to bear witness to the uniquely human potential at its best, which is to transform a personal tragedy into a triumph, to turn one's predicament into a human achievement. When we are no longer able to change a situation--just think of an incurable disease such as inoperable cancer--we are challenged to change ourselves.

A resilient person will find the positive aspect even in the worst of circumstances. Resiliency is the ability to persevere and rebound in the face of hardship, suffering, calamity, fears, distress, and stress. A resilient person takes the opportunity to leverage life's challenges and hardships as opportunities to grow, develop, and reinvent.

Resiliency rejuvenates your heart, mind, body, and soul and helps you to follow your life's purpose. Resiliency helps you to focus on what is important in life by clearing your heart, mind, body, and soul of junk and stress.

Resiliency is the ability to handle life's crises and to recover back to you normalcy. Resiliency helps you to overcome obstacles by helping you to manage stress and distress. Being resilient will help you to be unstoppable.

You need to build resiliency into your life. One way to build resiliency into your life is through the Power of the Positive. Resiliency allows you to be flexible and adaptive to life's challenges and uncertain situations. You need to prepare yourself physically, socially, spiritually, and emotionally to handle whatever life throws at you.

Building resiliency requires that you become proactive about your life. You need to start putting the effects you need in your life now so you can become more resilient. Being proactive enables you to prepare for future difficulties.

Gabrielle Giffords

On January 8, 2011, while meeting with her constituents, Congresswoman Gabrielle Giffords was shot outside the Safeway grocery store in Casas Adobes, Arizona, a suburban area northwest of Tucson. I know the area well since I grew up in Tucson and travelled that stretch of road quite often. It was shocking on two levels— one, Casas Adobes is a quiet area and two, I had met Gabby Giffords and wondered who would want to hurt her.

In February 2007, I met Congresswoman Gabrielle Giffords during a Congressional Delegation led by U.S. Senator Jon Kyl. This was her first visit to the Middle East as a Freshman Congresswoman newly sworn in on January

3, 2007. Since I was from Arizona and specifically from District 8, I wanted to meet the Delegation.

An important leadership role of a Command Chief is to speak directly to Congressional Delegations to pass on information on the health and morale of deployed personnel. This information may help when they make decisions in Congress based on what they see and hear while they are visiting.

Therefore, as expected, I took the opportunity to talk to her about our Wing and the morale of our Airmen. During my time in the desert I dealt with multiple congressional delegation visits, not all of them were pleasant, and at times, many of the visits seemed hurried. Congresswoman Gabrielle Giffords was different.

The thing that amazed me about Congresswoman Giffords was her graciousness and down to earth demeanor. However, the most refreshing part of the talk was that she actually listened and wanted to know more.

After I finished briefing her, she started asking the questions. She asked where I went to high school, where my family lived in Arizona, how long had I served in the Air Force, and what made me join. I could see that she really cared about what I was saying and who I was. She is a great woman.

After the shooting, I followed her progress and watched as she recovered. The one thing I realized about Gabby Giffords is that she is a fighter and very resilient.

Her positive determination to overcome life's obstacles and challenges is inspiring. She has not let a tragedy of life define her, she is defining her life. She is persevering to become better and stronger every day.

Gabby Giffords has maintained her optimism and focus on what matters most—life.

Train to Win

When the Air Force kicked off their new physical fitness program, I went out and established a run time to see where I was in relation to the new run times. Based on my run time, waist measurement, and the sit-ups I completed, I scored an 82.

Although that was acceptable, I was not satisfied with my score. I wanted to score in the 90s and preferably 92 or higher. I needed help to achieve my goal. I had two wingmen/mentors that helped me achieve my goals.

Kevin and Brian were my two mentors who helped me train to beat the standard, not just pass it. Three times a week Kevin, Brian, and I would run 3-4 miles to develop endurance and conditioning. Besides just running, we did wind sprints and staggered the running with a jog, run, and sprint cycle.

Over a period of 18 weeks, my time went from 13:12 to 11:42. We continued to train up to the first physical assessment. On the day of the run, I finished with an 11:24 and scored a 92 on the physical assessment. We continued to run three times a week and competed in 5ks throughout the year.

The next year during my run, I finished with a 10:31. After the physical assessment, I left and went to Altus Air Force Base, Oklahoma. Since I no longer had the benefit of my two mentors, I needed something or someone to push me to train and develop for the next year.

I needed to create an effect that would help me achieve my desired outcome. To help me continue to challenge myself and to achieve my goals, I set up the Command Chief Run for each month and gave t-shirts for anyone who could beat the Chief.

In my first six months I handed out 56 t-shirts to Airmen who beat my time. I continued this run for the two years I was assigned to Altus and my run times fell to 10:02 and finally 9:49. Mentoring and constant challenging myself to stay in the 90s helped me to stay fit throughout my Air Force career.

Life is just like that example. It requires you to keep training, developing, and growing yourself to win. It also requires you to put a proactive effect in place to achieve your desired outcome. Here are five tips to help improve your resiliency.

- Do not become a recluse during crisis or tragedy. Being resilient is not a one-person deal. You need life-affirming relationships with close family members and friends to be resilient and healthy. When catastrophe hits you, the worst thing you can do is to seek solitude. You need people in your life to lean on during times of trouble.

- Keep the situation in perspective. Don't let the tragedy cloud your judgment or outlook on life. Seek to understand the tragedy, how it will affect your life, and do not let it control your life. Keep your eyes focused on getting through the tragedy and do not be overcome. Be an overcomer!

- Maintain your optimism. Despite the difficulty you are facing, keep a positive mindset. It will help you be resilient and help you avoid feeling negative. As you progress through the difficulty, focus on your strengths and abilities to get you through.

- Maintain a healthy lifestyle and take care of yourself. Do what you need to do to stay healthy. Get enough sleep, exercise daily, and eat healthy food. A healthy mind and body will help you be resilient and adaptive.

POWER #4
Trust, Respect, and Integrity

The Power of Trust, Respect, and Integrity is a life affirming value. A person who is open and honest today never has to remember the lie told yesterday. Authenticity means a person is accountable and responsible for their actions, words, and decisions.

Why are integrity, trust, and respect important? People need to trust, respect, and believe in you. Mutual trust and respect is necessary if you want to live with integrity. Integrity is the bedrock foundation upon which all successful relationships are built.

Being a person of integrity requires a conscious decision. Integrity is key to building and sustaining trust. Trust and respect begins with a solid foundation of lifelong integrity and congruency. Trust and respect are preconditions for open communication and authentic dialogue.

Your walk and your talk need to match. In his book, *The 8th Habit: From Effectiveness to Greatness*, Stephen Covey says, "Trust is the key to all relationships." Relationships are held together by a level of trust and mutual respect that each person in the relationship has for one another.

A person of genuine and authentic character is trustworthy. Building trust takes time and commitment. Trust is a vital component of your success and is the very heart of every relationship. Trust is a relationship established between you and another person.

In each relationship, you take a risk when you trust another person. You are taking the risk that the other person is trustworthy. When you build your relationships on integrity, respect, and trust, you are banking on that risk and letting the other person know that they are trustworthy.

When you create an environment of integrity, trust, and respect, you enlarge, empower, and value each person. It is all about building and sustaining relationships.

In addition, relationships are built upon trust and respect which is all about your character. Integrity means living by your word, keeping your promises, and over-delivering in everything you do. To be truly authentic your words and actions are the same.

POWER #5

Humor and Humility

Why are humor and humility so powerful in your life? Humility and humor helps you to perfect your outlook on life. Humor allows you to express and strengthen your humility by keeping things in perspective. Humor allows you to not take yourself too seriously and helps you keep yourself from becoming too prideful.

A key trait of a humble nature is learning to laugh at yourself and keep yourself grounded in reality. Mark Twain said, "Humor is mankind's greatest blessing" and C.S. Lewis said, "Humor is…the all-consoling and…the all-excusing, grace of life." Humor helps you to become a positive and humble person by helping you to have joy in your heart. Humor establishes a positive emotional climate for your life.

Humility is your self-confidence in your abilities and capabilities and a clear understanding of your self-worth. C.S. Lewis said, "True humility is not thinking less of yourself; it is thinking of yourself less." and Charles H. Spurgeon said, "Humility is to make a right estimate of oneself." Both of these are good definitions on humility.

These two traits allow you to be more adaptive in the world. Humility helps you keep your life in perspective and it helps you keep yourself in perspective. Humor helps to ease your problems, inspires daily optimism, and keeps you grounded.

POWER #6
Forgiveness and Grace

Forgiving yourself and forgiving others are two important parts of the Power of Forgiveness. To be very honest, forgiving yourself is much tougher than forgiving someone else. Why?...Because each of us at times carries around feelings of self-blame for something that happened in our past. If these negative feelings go unresolved, they bury themselves deep into your core and have a way of affecting your daily lives.

Forgiving yourself is a vital action of creating a positive mindset and outlook for your life. It unleashes you to move toward a positive future by releasing yourself from a negative past. Forgiving others allows you to move on and re-channel the anger and hurt into something positive.

Remember: your past mistakes most likely made you who you are today. So do not look at them as mistakes but as pathways to your future.

Forgiving yourself helps you to resolve deep-set anger, feelings of resentment, feelings of despair, and a lack of self-esteem.

Forgiving yourself also helps you to unleash your life from sadness, hurt, and blame. It also helps with your overall physical and mental health. Here are some ways to forgive yourself and others

- Start with forgiving yourself and stop letting your past continue to haunt your present
- Learn to value who you are and can become
- Be thankful for what you do have and see the good in your life now
- Focus your thoughts on the positive when negativity arises
- Think about how you have forgiven others in the past
- Forgive others for their transgressions
- Your mistakes do not define you
- Distance yourself from negative people
- Be an agent of hope and mercy
- Bestow grace and forgive

POWER #7

Faith, Hope, And Love

For there are these three things that endure: Faith, Hope and Love, but the greatest of these is Love.
Corinthians 1 13:13

The power cycle begins with the Power of Believing, but ends with the Power of Faith, Hope, and Love. Of all the powers discussed, this is the most important. Why?

Because where there is no faith, there is hopelessness and despair. When you lose hope, you lose yourself and your reason to live on purpose. When you lose yourself, you lose your love for life. In everything, do not give up hope.

The young Soldier at the Brooks Army Medical Center who gave up hope on his life found this power when he turned to his faith. Through his faith, he found hope again. When he found hope, he loved his life again. When he loved his life again, he believed in himself and his life.

Faith, Hope, and Love help you to believe that your circumstances, no matter how dark and gloomy it feels, will get better. By having faith in your heart, when you go through times of turmoil, without a doubt, you have Hope.

It is a real belief that despite the chaos that is surrounding you, you have a quiet resolve that it will pass and you will press on toward the prize. It is a belief and awareness that you will face the challenge and come out stronger, better, and full of life. I believe that the greatest hope we have is that God created us to be a message of faith, hope, and love to the world.

Summary

The Power Cycle are those actions or effects that you can do in your life to make it unstoppable. Each area helps you to fulfill your purpose, vision, and mission in life and helps to increase the positives in your life. The Power Cycle is a way of recalibrating your life and refocusing you to living "on purpose."

Live Life Freely!

REFLECTION TIME

Give yourself some quiet time—20 minutes to start and reflect on who you truly are.

Personal Assessment

Review the statements and select the answer that best fits how you assess your life at this moment.

I believe in my capabilities and myself.

1 2 3 4 5 6 7 8 9 10

I have self-confidence in my life.

1 2 3 4 5 6 7 8 9 10

I am not afraid to stand up for my principles and values.

1 2 3 4 5 6 7 8 9 10

I have the moral courage in my life to live out my values despite what others may do.

1 2 3 4 5 6 7 8 9 10

I have learned to be resilient in my life.

1 2 3 4 5 6 7 8 9 10

I keep things in perspective.

1 2 3 4 5 6 7 8 9 10

I remain optimistic despite life's challenges.

1 2 3 4 5 6 7 8 9 10

I believe in hope versus despair.

1 2 3 4 5 6 7 8 9 10

I have forgiven myself for my past transgressions in order move forward in my life.

1 2 3 4 5 6 7 8 9 10

Self-Assessment Analysis

10-39 Points – You need to increase your self-awareness and self-efficacy. Take the time to do a deep dive on yourself to find out who you are and how to improve your life. If you want your life to be a masterpiece, you need to be the master of the pieces of your life.

40-70 Points – You have a good understanding of who you are but have areas that you need to grow and develop. Which area of your life do you need to improve? What effects do you need to implement to produce better outcomes?

71-89 Points – You are well on your way to being unstoppable in your life. You are living an abundant life and you understand the Principle of the Harvest. You know your true self and you are living your true purpose. Keep your eye on the prize and keep pressing forward.

90-100 Points – You are unstoppable. You are the Master of the Pieces of your life. However, do not stop now. You need to continue to grow, develop, and continually reinvent yourself.

UNSTOPPABLE TAKEAWAYS

Be Resilient

You need to build resiliency into your life. Resiliency is a critical element that allows you to come back stronger than ever after crisis and chaos.

Be Courageous

You were meant to be courageous and live your life purposefully. Courage is the foundation and the backbone of your life. You need to live your life boldly, confidently, and with courage.

Be Trustworthy

Trust, integrity, and respect means following your values, beliefs, and purpose and valuing those around you.
Integrity + Respect = Trustworthiness

ARE YOU BREATHING A.I.R?

Take a moment to reflect on your life. Look at the chart of actions, impacts, and results and use it as a road map to guide you on your Journey. What is your next step in your expedition?

ACTIONS	IMPACT
• Be Courageous • Be Confident • Believe in yourself • Be resilient • Forgive others	• Increased stamina • Hopeful outlook • Trustworthy
RESULTS	
• A Powerful and Resilient life!	

CHAPTER 10

THE UNSTOPPABLE LIFE

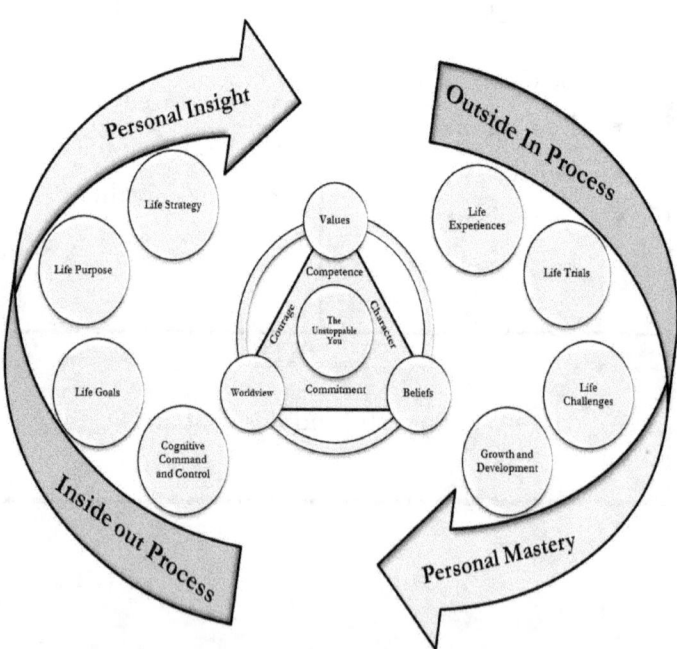

"Hardships often prepare ordinary people for an extraordinary destiny"
C.S. Lewis

My Grandfather

My grandfather was a Marine in WWII. That is probably all I would need to say to tell you what kind of man he was. However, you would miss who he really was. He was much more than a Marine. He was proud of his service, he was proud of his nation, but most of all he loved his family. My grandfather was one of my heroes as I grew up.

He was 8 feet tall and had arms the size of trees. At least that is what I thought when I was 5 years old. If you met my grandfather, you would never forget him. My grandfather had an indomitable spirit and a huge heart. He made an impact on you right away. As I grew up my respect for my grandfather grew.

I loved who he was and what he stood for. He, along with other family members who served, is the reason I enlisted. They were my giants. When cancer struck my grandfather, he fought back like a Marine. He gave it no quarter.

My grandfather fought cancer twice in his life and fought back both times. He believed in Hope and fighting back against an enemy. However, cancer has a way of taking a hero and reducing their superhuman powers.

Because of cancer, my grandfather could no longer lift a truck over his head or break a tree with his bare hands, but his zest for life and the fire in his eyes was present. I was deployed to Taif, Saudi Arabia, when my hero went home to be with his Savior, but his indomitable spirit lives on in the legacy of his family.

He was Unstoppable!

Unstoppable Life Effects

What does your unstoppable life look like? It is different for each person. Remember, you are unique so your unstoppable life will be unique to you.

Creating an unstoppable life is not easy, in fact, you are not entitled to an unstoppable life, it will be your hard work that creates it. However, the return on your life investment is worth it.

Unshakeable Purpose

To be unstoppable you need to have fundamenta inconcussa. Fundamenta inconcussa is Latin for unshakable foundation. Aristotle called this his first principles or his self-evident truths.

In order to lead your life and be unstoppable you need to know your first principles or your self-evident truths. You need to know who you are, what you stand for, what you believe in, what your values are, and what you will stand firm for in your life.

Once you know your first principles, you create an unshakable life foundation and you create an unshakable purpose in life. Your purpose is the Why of your life. Why you are driven in a certain direction, why you act in the way you do, why you believe what you believe, and why you live your life.

An unshakeable purpose makes you unstoppable because you have fundamenta inconcussa. Your key to living an unstoppable life is to keep your purpose in focus, on fire, and unshakeable. You must be committed to your own path, stand firm in your convictions, and live each day on purpose.

New Vision

Everything begins with your vision for life. You are the founder of your vision. Your vision begins by creating a compelling future from your desire. It is your desire to live an unstoppable and abundant life.

Your success begins with your ability to envision a bright and prosperous future by establishing a vision that excites you. That is the power of vision.

Your vision creates a sense of purpose and inspires and motivates you every day. You must be able to build a clear and inspiring vision. Your vision provides you clarity and focus and clearly defines your strategy for the future.

Vision allows you the freedom and liberty to create, design, and choose outcomes that will make your life successful and unstoppable.

Stretch Your Life

Get out of your comfort zone. Your comfort zone is a self-made prison that keeps you contained. Do not allow your fear of control and fear of failure define who you are. A fear of the unknown will keep you stuck forever. You need to move beyond your comfort zone to stretch and grow your life.

The true magic of your life is beyond the limits of your comfort zone. It is where you can grow, develop, and experience a life that expands your horizons beyond what you thought was possible.

Run toward a future that taps into your full potential. Push back on your comfort zone and push into life.

Take the Risk

Living is a risk. Live Life, Live Now! You need to embrace the risk that will create the life you want. Life is a continuous gamble and risk. You cannot live your life in fear. You need to take the risk and face your fears in order to live an unstoppable life. In everything you do, you stake your life and your very own existence to move forward.

Risk is what you perceive it to be. You can perceive it to be uncertainty or you can perceive it as an adventure waiting for you. You need to live in this world like there's no tomorrow. Take the risk to dream. Take the risk to go places you have only dreamed of going. Take the risk to conquer your fears. Take the risk to live in the great adventure called life. It is your life, take the risk to become unstoppable.

Overcomer Mindset

Whatever life throws at you, you can overcome it. Success in any aspect of life starts with your mindset. Negative beliefs, concepts, and thoughts are like powerful headwinds throwing you off course and halting your forward progress.

To overcome you need a positive outlook and life-affirming mindset. You can overcome life's challenges and your fears if you have an unyielding belief in yourself, your abilities, and your capability to make an impact. Be an overcomer in your life and face down your challenges and your fears.

Pay the Price

You reap what your sow. Take the time early in your life to understand that the principles of preparing the soil and reaping a harvest are important concepts. You can pay the price now to reap the rewards later. Self-development exacts a price in hard work, commitment, and perseverance in order to achieve your personal goals. Nevertheless, the best investment you can ever make is to invest in yourself, your talents, and your skills. There is always a price to pay in time, money, and sweat, but it rarely exceeds the return of investment in your personal development.

Put it in Perspective

Much of life's experience depends on your attitude and your perceptions. Putting your life into perspective is a valuable way to lead yourself. Life is short and by developing new insights and a fresh perspective, you will expand the way you see the possibilities in your career, life, and relationships. Your perceptions create your reality, so make sure you keep them positive.

All-in Action

To be unstoppable you need to be "All-in" with 100% of your effort in life. In order to truly "go all out" and make unprecedented progress, you must make the decision at a core level to hold nothing back. You must take a good look at your life and decide that nothing is going to stand in your way of success. All-in is taking ownership of your life with confidence and commitment.

Believe in Yourself

Take the time every morning to reaffirm your belief in yourself. Define yourself. Believe in yourself. If you do not believe in yourself, then it does not matter how talented and gifted you are or how big your dreams are. You will never achieve them.

If you want to succeed, you have to believe in yourself. You must have an overwhelming belief in yourself. Believe in yourself, in the power you have. Believe in the strength that you have within your very core and it will fortify you every step of your life.

Lead Yourself Daily

Every day begins as a tabula rasa, or blank slate, for you to create your life's masterpiece. How you take advantage of that canvas begins with how you start and manage your day. Each day you have an opportunity to choose how you want to use the day.

You can be successful one day or one decision at a time. You must inspire and lead yourself daily. You need the self-discipline to follow through with daily decisions and commitments. Use each day to create your masterpiece.

Exceed Expectations

Never settle for second best in your life. Learn to exceed your own expectations by striving to become the very best person you can become. If you want to see success in your career, avoid merely meeting expectations. Exceed the expectations every time you do something. The expectations you exceed today become the seeds for new opportunities in the future.

Learn Something Every Day

Your mind is your greatest asset and must be developed and grown every day. Your body requires food every day in order to thrive and survive, so does your mind. You need to take time every day to read and develop your mind. Add a new skill or talent. Add a new capability. Learn something new that enriches and grows your life on a daily basis. By learning something new each day you keep your mind expanding.

Intentional Future

You create your future with your intentions and actions. Intention is the mindful action of determining your future outcomes today. The F(X) Model is concerned with creating the effects to determine your outcomes. When you are intentional with your choices and decisions, you start creating your future.

By intentionally creating your outcomes, you will find new ways to create life opportunities. Dream big and create a compelling and inspiring vision for your future.

Forward Thinking

You must be future-oriented and forward thinking. Part of the unstoppable life is foresight. In order to be better prepared to take advantage of events and challenges, you need to envision and anticipate the future. Foresight is not predicting the future, but anticipating how your future might unfold.

This will help you become prepared to deal with a difficult circumstance. You must anticipate the 2nd, 3rd, and 4th order of effects of your decisions to take advantage of your possible future. Understanding and assessing where you are today will help you create foresight.

Escape

Now is the time to reinvent yourself and develop a new plan of action. Now is the time to create new actions and practices that are focused on growth and development in your personal and professional life. Now is the time for rebirth, to unleash your leadership potential, and ignite your passion to lead. It is time for you to break out and discover your new life.

You must Fight the Good Fight

Fight the good fight of the faith. Take hold of the eternal life to which you were called when you made your good confession in the presence of many witnesses.
1 Timothy 6:12

Your life is worth fighting for each day. Your life is full of potential and possibilities.. Each morning you must make a choice to live your life or live the life the world wants you to live. You must make that choice, do you compromise or do live authentically?

When you compromise your beliefs, values, dreams, and aspirations to fit in to the world's expectations, you die a little inside every day. When you compromise a little each day, soon you are no longer you. You are now the creation the world wants you to be versus the unstoppable you that you should be.

If you want to live an unstoppable life, you must be honest with yourself and Fight the Good Fight every day. You are worth it. When you sell your soul for 30 pieces of silver, you sell your unstoppable life too cheaply. Your life is worth more than silver or gold.

You only get one chance to live your life, live it to the fullest of your purpose and Fight the Good Fight every day. Fight to take your life back and fight to have the world accept you for who you are and who you are becoming. You are the key to your destiny, do not turn your keys over to someone else. When life pushes you, you need to push back harder. Never surrender and do not give up on yourself. Fight every minute of every day, take a stand, and fight for who you are!

Living Your Unstoppable Legacy

I believe each of us is unstoppable. You can do anything you desire if you choose to pay the price and make the choices. We have a finite time here to make a difference and to leave some sort of legacy. If you knew how much time you had to spend on earth, would you make different decisions? Would you stop wasting time? Would you take yourself more serious?

Legacy is the embodiment your life. Each time your build your legacy it is an ending and a beginning. It is constant growth, development, and reinvent of your life at each phase. You create your legacy as you progress through each phase of your personal and professional career.

Your Unstoppable legacy grows with every new skill, talent, ability, and capability that you acquire. Your Unstoppable legacy grows with each new experience, each new risk, and each new idea. Your Unstoppable legacy grows each time you grow, develop, and reinvent yourself.

Your Unstoppable legacy grows with each new relationship, each new alliance, and each time your share your life. Your Unstoppable legacy grows each time you teach, coach, and mentor someone to live an Unstoppable Life.

What will your legacy be? When people read your life story, will they read about an unstoppable life of adventure, challenges, and a life lived to its fullest? Or, will they read a story of a life unlived, a life of mediocrity, and a life of comfort zone living? The choice is yours to make, the journey is yours to take.

My journey has not always been positive and easy. I have had my share of the big three--mistakes, failures, and setbacks. To be truthfully honest, I have learned more from those big three than I have from my successes. Mistakes, failures, and setbacks made me want to strive harder to achieve my success and it taught me valuable lessons and principles along the pathway.

The lessons became my stepping-stones of growth and the principles became what I call the unstoppable self-development process. The Unstoppable process has helped me shape, live, and forge my life. It can do the same for your life if you are committed and have the discipline to apply the principles.

As stated earlier in the book, everything starts with you. You are the one that brings your dreams to creation. You are the founder of your past, present, and future you. You possess the unstoppable power to create a positive and amazing life.

There is virtually no limit of who you can become, what you can do, and what you can become with an unstoppable belief in yourself. Choosing to live an Unstoppable Life is not easy, but is rewarding.

Change starts from the inside. You must want to change. You must have the desire to change. You must be committed to the change. You have to work hard to change. Change may take time and patience before you see the effects of your change. Do not give up on change.

The degree to which you can realize your dreams is

contingent on you taking responsibility and never giving up on your life. No one can live your life or make your decisions. Living an unstoppable life is a choice and you must make the choice to be unstoppable.

Take a moment to reflect what you have learned so far in this book.

- To live an Unstoppable Life you must live inspired and believe in who you are. You must live daily with purpose, passion, persistence, and perseverance.

- To live an Unstoppable Life you must take charge of your life and live congruently with your purpose, values, beliefs, and worldview.

- To live an Unstoppable Life you must be committed to continuously grow, develop, and reinvent yourself.

- To live an Unstoppable Life you must live fearlessly and uncompromisingly.

- To live an Unstoppable Life you must live your true self.

An Unstoppable Declaration

Time is the coin of your life. It is the only coin you have, and only you can determine how it will be spent. Be careful lest you let other people spend it for you.
Carl Sandburg

On July 4, 1776, John Hancock, John Adams, Samuel Adams, Thomas Jefferson, Benjamin Franklin, and 51 Founding Fathers signed off the Declaration of

Independence. In their bold stroke of the pen, they set the course for the birth of the United States of America and transformed 13 separate colonies into a nation.

Those that signed the Declaration of Independence solemnly pledged to one another and to the new nation that they would fight at all costs. They pledged "their lives, their fortunes, and their sacred honor." This document declared to the World that we were Free and Independent:

> We hold these truths to be self-evident, that all men are created equal, that they are endowed by their Creator with certain unalienable Rights, that among these are Life, Liberty and the pursuit of Happiness.

> That to secure these rights, Governments are instituted among Men, deriving their just powers from the consent of the governed, that whenever any Form of Government becomes destructive of these ends, it is the Right of the People to alter or to abolish it, and to institute new Government, laying its foundation on such principles and organizing its powers in such form, as to them shall seem most likely to affect their Safety and Happiness.

The words of the Declaration of Independence are powerful and are, in my opinion, the keys to being unstoppable. We are all created equal. We are all brought into the world the same way and have the same opportunity to make our life what we want it to be.

If our life is not turning out the way we want it to we can change it. Thomas Hobbes in his book *Leviathan*, states

> Nature hath made men so equal, in the faculties of body and mind, as that though there be found one man sometimes manifestly stronger in body, or of

quicker mind than another; yet when all is reckoned together, the difference between man and man is not so considerable, as that one man can thereupon claim to himself any benefit, to which another may not pretend, as well as he….From this equality of ability, ariseth equality of hope in the attaining of our Ends.

I believe we each have the same chance to succeed in life. It does not mean each of us will have the same outcome though. You need to choose what you want out of life to be successful.

Each of us defines success differently. Each of us has to live the life we were given and live it to fulfill our purpose. You have a distinctive set of strengths, skills, talents, and gifts which will help you achieve your desired success. You also will face different challenges that you will have to overcome to achieve your success.

Our unalienable rights are not a gift from Government but from our Creator. We can be who we want to be not because our Government tells us we can, but because our Creator has endowed us with a life of possibilities.

One way to declare your unstoppable life is through your own Declaration to the World. A declaration is your way of declaring to the World that you are going to fight for your unstoppable life and that you are not afraid to let them know. It is a way to let others know that you choose to live your life unstoppable and unafraid.

It is your way to put a line in the sand and take a stand for your life. The declaration on the next few pages is an example of a declaration of an unstoppable life.

Declaration of a Unstoppable Life

When in the Course of living my life, it becomes necessary for me to reinvent myself. I hold this truth to be self-evident, that I was created equal, that I am endowed by my Creator with certain unalienable Rights, that among these are Life, Liberty and the Pursuit of Happiness—That to secure these rights, I must take charge of my life.

That whenever any part of my life becomes destructive, it is my Right to alter or to abolish it, and to institute a new way of life, laying its foundation on my values, beliefs, and principles and organizing it in such a way as to affect my life's outcomes.

PURPOSE STATEMENT: To live an inspired life, to live on purpose, and to live unstoppable. I want to live my life and give my everything!

VISION STATEMENT: I will live an authentic and inspiring life fully awake and alive choosing to create the outcomes in my life.

MISSION STATEMENT: To establish and live a balanced life encompassing my family life, professional career, and my personal growth and development goals. To foster an inspirational environment which breathes life into my family and others. To use my voice to live my Faith and to live for love.

I choose to live an inspired and unstoppable life.

I choose to build my life upon solid values and beliefs and to live them out daily.

I choose to use my voice and stand up for what I believe inside.

I choose to follow Christ as my Savior.

I choose to live my life to speak life into others and not destroy their lives with my words.

I choose to love unconditionally.

I choose to envision and communicate an inspiring vision and clearly define a strategy for the future.

I choose to continuously grow, develop, and reinvent myself to become better every day.

I choose to be responsible and accountable for my life's decisions and actions.

I choose to passionately pursue my purpose.

I choose to have an overcomer mindset.

I choose to be a lifelong learner who is agile, adaptive and reflective, that learns from experiences, training, development, successes, and failures.

I choose to invest in my capabilities, talents, and character.

I choose to achieve mastery of my life and leadership to lead and dare greatly.

I choose to improvise, adapt, and overcome as rapidly as the current pace of change.

I choose to be flexible and resilient in my response to crisis and to change.

I choose to be multi-culturally astute and understand different countries, cultures, religions, and worldviews

I choose to be a master at networking, relationships, and alliance building.

I, therefore, appealing to the Supreme Judge of the orld for the rectitude of my intentions, do, in the Name, and by Authority of myself, solemnly publish and declare, I choose to live an unstoppable life. Furthermore, for the support of this Declaration, with a firm reliance on the protection of divine Providence, I pledge my sacred Honor.

Summary

In the same fashion the Founding Fathers of America declared themselves free and unstoppable, you need to declare to the world the you are free to be unstoppable. It is your choice to live unstoppable. Be bold in your life and declare yourself unstoppable.

> # Live Life Unstoppable!

REFLECTION TIME

Give yourself some quiet time—20 minutes to start and reflect on your life.

Self-assessment

Review the statements and select the answer that best fits how you assess your life at this moment.

I believe in my capability to create outcomes for my life.
    1 2 3 4 5 6 7 8 9 10

I want to create a masterpiece of my life.
    1 2 3 4 5 6 7 8 9 10

I am ready to implement the effects I need to change.
    1 2 3 4 5 6 7 8 9 10

I have established personal goals for my life.
    1 2 3 4 5 6 7 8 9 10

I have learned to take a proactive approach to my life.
    1 2 3 4 5 6 7 8 9 10

I am willing to pay the price to create a positive life.
    1 2 3 4 5 6 7 8 9 10

I have established goals in all eight areas of self-development.
    1 2 3 4 5 6 7 8 9 10

I willingly assess all areas of my life each year.
    1 2 3 4 5 6 7 8 9 10

I know my roadblocks and obstacles.
    1 2 3 4 5 6 7 8 9 10

I am ready to use a disciplined approach to my life.
    1 2 3 4 5 6 7 8 9 10

Self-Assessment Analysis

10-39 Points – You need to increase your self-awareness and self-efficacy. Take the time to do a deep dive on yourself to find out who you are and how to improve your life. If you want your life to be a masterpiece, you need to be the master of the pieces of your life.

40-70 Points – You have a good understanding of who you are but have areas that you need to grow and develop. Which area of your life do you need to improve? What effects do you need to implement to produce better outcomes?

71-89 Points – You are well on your way to being unstoppable in your life. You are living an abundant life and you understand the Principle of the Harvest. You know your true self and you are living your true purpose. Keep your eye on the prize and keep pressing forward.

90-100 Points – You are unstoppable. You are the Master of the Pieces of your life. However, do not stop now. You need to continue to grow, develop, and continually reinvent yourself.

UNSTOPPABLE TAKEAWAYS

An Unshakeable Belief

You need to have an unshakeable belief in yourself and who you are. To live an unstoppable life you must believe that you are here on purpose and add value to the world. To live an unstoppable life you must believe in your talents, skills, capabilities, and gifts.

ARE YOU BREATHING A.I.R?

Take a moment to reflect on your life. Look at the chart of actions, impacts, and results and use it as a road map to guide you on your Journey. What is your next step in your expedition?

ACTIONS	IMPACT
<ul><li>Declare yourself to be Unstoppable</li><li>Unshakeable belief in yourself</li><li>Unstoppable Attitude</li></ul>	<ul><li>Transformed Life</li><li>Transformed Attitude</li><li>Transformed Outlook</li></ul>
RESULTS	
<ul><li>Unstoppable and Unleashed Inspired Life!</li></ul>	

Conclusion

He replied, "Because you have so little faith. Truly I tell you, if you have faith as small as a mustard seed, you can say to this mountain, 'Move from here to there,' and it will move. Nothing will be impossible for you."
Matthew 17:20

Here we are again at that fork in the road. Have you made your choice for which road you will take? Do you choose to live inspired or are you already retired?

Do you choose to risk it all or play it safe? On this marathon and lifetime journey, choosing the right road will make all the difference in your life? It all begins with the sine qua non or your essential choice.

Do you choose to travel the easy path of good enough, comfort zones, and status quo?

OR…do you choose to find your voice and your life and travel the road of discovery, of learning, of development, of growth, and enjoy an unrelenting adventure for excellence? The marathon will be demanding and inspiring. It will require persistence and perseverance, and it will take personal courage and resilience.

However, most significantly, on this marathon you will discover a meaningful and enriching life. One that you have championed by choosing to live it. The outcome of this unstoppable and true self-life is that you will leave a legacy of inspired and enriched people in your wake.

Life Unstoppable

One of my favorite self-development/leadership development movies is *A Knight's Tale* with Heath Ledger.

Although I used this story in my first book, its importance cannot be overstated.

To find your true self requires awareness and action. The story is about personal change, self-awareness, success, failure, experience, and growth and development. It is also about a disciplined approach to development, taking responsibility for your life, and continuously reinventing yourself as you grow and develop.

A poignant part of the movie shows how young William gets his start in which you see a father taking his son to be a Knight's page. His father wanted him to have a different life than a thatcher, so he lets his son become a page for a Knight.

His father was his first mentor and he taught him his values and beliefs, and helped to shape his worldview. He also taught him the value of hard work by teaching him the craft of roof thatching.

Thatching was hard work, and by learning this craft, he developed discipline and an attitude of service. If he stayed, he would only be a thatcher, nothing more nothing less. As they part his father says, "this is all I can do for you…watch and learn…go and change your stars."

This is the first trial for the young leader. He is leaving his first mentor and now is under the tutelage of Sir Ector, his new mentor. He quickly learns the importance of self-reliance, how to follow, and how to be a member of a team.

The next three big life lessons for the leader are decision-making, risk taking, and being courageous. In the movie, the old Knight dies just before he is about to win the tournament.

The young leader, who has gone from being a page to a squire, has grown up in the mentoring of a Knight and his team. He takes a risk and decides he will enter the tournament and fight.

He steps up as a leader to take care of his team in order for all of them to survive. His courage to face the overwhelming challenge changes the fate of him and that of the team.

The win inspires him and gives him confidence he did not have prior to the challenge. From this newfound confidence in his ability, he decides to become a Knight. His teammates realize he is not ready and he needs more training and development to meet the challenges of the volatile, uncertain, complex, and ambiguous (VUCA) environment.

After a period of training and development, the team heads to their first tournament, and along the way they realize they cannot fight under the old knight's name and must invent a new name and leadership persona. This is the first time we see the young leader reinvent himself.

He is no longer William; he is a Knight!

He has begun the change process. As he competes in tournaments, he gains the professional experience he needs to be a Knight, he gains confidence and self-awareness in his personal life, and as he becomes a Knight, he gains wisdom in his leadership as a team leader.

Part of this change process is the issue of the old armor and new armor. The old armor of the old Knight is the leadership style and teachings of the status quo. As William develops and grows as a leader, his style and his tactics develop, he breaks out of the shell of his old mentor and becomes his own leader.

He puts on the armor of his new leadership, which helps him meet the challenges of the VUCA environment he is encountering. The new armor is light, mobile, and allows him greater range of movement against his competitors. He is light, lean, and lethal. He has reinvented himself again. He is ready for the new challenges of his new life. The student has surpassed his two mentors. As he continues to meet the challenges of the tournaments, he grows from thinking that he is a Knight to becoming a Knight.

He has emerged from being a thatcher's son, a page, and a squire, to the top of his profession. He is now the expert. His true leadership emerges when his identity is discovered and he is about to be arrested.

Instead of running from the challenges and adversity, he stands his ground and proclaims that he will not run and that he is a Knight. He accepts what is about to happen to him and accepts the consequences for his decisions.

Through his trials, development, and experiences he has become the leader he envisioned himself to be and he learns the value of perseverance and persistence.

There is no turning back for him…he chose to **be UNSTOPPABLE!** He is a Knight in the oldest tradition--chivalrous, noble, and authentic. The Prince of England knights him because he recognizes his true leadership, his true purpose, and his ability to inspire.

Sir William has completed the transformation of his life. The story does not end there though. The new Sir William needs to face the adversity of those who still think of him as just a "thatcher."

In his final joust he is victorious over what the world can throw at him because of what his father taught him—his values and his beliefs. Through his disciplined approach and desire to become better, he became victorious in life, his career, and leadership. In the end, he "changed his stars."

So....What's Next?

So what is down the road for you? How do you keep the momentum going and inertia at bay? How do you keep on this unstoppable life? I recommend, if you have not done so yet, go back to each exercise and start completing them.

This will help you to define and refine yourself for your marathon. If you have already completed the exercises, I recommend you take the time and review them every month for encouragement and progress. I further recommend if you want to do a deep dive an discover more about yourself get the You are Unstoppable Participant's Guide and the 70 Day Jumpstart Life Journal.

Another way that will help you reinforce the ideas and concepts in your life is to take the time to teach the principles to someone else. Take one chapter at a time and lead your family, a friend, or even a co-worker through the book.

Use the book as a way to encourage, inspire others, and encourage them to grow, develop, and reinvent themselves. This will help you to start leaving a legacy of inspired and enriched people in your path.

Living your L.I.F.E. on Mission

In the Introduction of the book, I introduced you to the L.I.F.E concept and why I choose to write books with these four key words. The acronym L.I.F.E. stands for Leadership, Inspiration, Faith, and Empowerment. You can live your life on the L.I.F.E mission by taking the time to look inside yourself each day to see if you are living in accordance with your purpose, values, and worldview. Staying congruent is the gift of introspection. It allows you to continue to fulfill your purpose by refocusing yourself.

Leadership

Leadership is an inside-out process and is shaped by your values, character, choices, opportunities, experiences, and your worldview. Leading with your purpose and your core values ensures your life and leadership are congruent. As an authentic leader, you inspire yourself and others to greatness.

This is the key to leading yourself. You have to know who you are before you know where you can go. Your life's purpose begins with the self-knowledge of why you are here and what you are living to fulfill. Go the extra mile in your life. Do not settle for your best; strive to achieve your greatest.

The extra mile mindset will help you succeed in life and in your work. People will notice when you do more than you were asked to do. When you exceed expectations, you are creating more possibilities for your future.

Inspiration

Living on purpose and serving a higher purpose breathes life into you every day and gives you the desire to reach your goals. You need to live each day congruently by living within your beliefs and values.

Unleashing your inspired life starts with living your life's purpose. As you grow and develop, you assimilate new ideas, new concepts, and new skills that change you from the "as-is" model to the "to-be" model. You are constantly reinventing yourself as growth and development brings new life into your abilities, talents, and gifts, and by discarding the old. Keep moving from the old self to the new self. You will marvel at the new creation that you can become.

Seek to inspire yourself and your people every day. Take time to breathe life into yourself and those around you by being an inspiration. Being inspirational is a choice you make every day and make throughout your day. You can choose to breathe life into others or you can choose to extinguish hope.

Faith

Life is an adventure of self-discovery and discovering life. Faith in yourself and faith in God provides you the strength you need each day to put your foot on the path and begin each new day in awe and wonder.

Using your faith as your measuring standard, you can create your life's vision to achieve your dreams and goals. You must also have faith in yourself and believe you are unstoppable. Take the time to see the possibilities that lie before you. When you take the time to see the possibilities that the future can hold for you it creates a momentum in your life to succeed and achieve your dreams.

Seeing the future possibilities is a powerful positive motivator. The first step in making the impossible the possible is faith in your talents, gifts, and mostly, faith in yourself. By focusing on mindfulness, you can see the possibilities in your life. Take time to see the possibilities in your life.

Empowerment

Your greatest power in life is the liberty to choose. It is the liberty to choose what you want to do with your life, where you want to go, and what you want to become. No one can take this power away from you; it is yours alone. You can do what you want to do; you can be who you want to be.

You can live an empowered life through your decisions and choices each day. Your choices determine your attitude and your altitude. When you follow a strong and empowering purpose, you will live, think, and act on purpose and within your purpose. Life is a journey not a destination.

You do not achieve the prize by reaching for what is in your grasp. You need to stretch yourself, get out of your comfort zones, and reach far beyond what you can see. Keep your eye on the prize of life--the people you meet, the experiences you have, the beauty you see, and most of all, the life you lead. Strive to live your life inspiring people.

What is Your Story?

In the beginning of the book I stated that leadership principles are timeless, unfortunately, we are not. We have a finite time here to make a difference and to leave some sort of legacy. If you knew how much time you had to spend on earth would you make different decisions? Would you stop wasting time? Would you take yourself more serious?

You are Unstoppable is about the difference you make in yourself every day. It is about the effects and outcomes you want for your life. It is about taking responsibility for your growth and development.. It is being serious with your approach to developing yourself to be ready for whatever life throws at you. You are Unstoppable is not giving in or giving up on yourself. The time is now to radically change your life, career, and leadership.

Discover your purpose and passionately pursue it

The first thing you need to as a leader is to awaken the leader within you. It is about discovering you true self. It is about seizing control of your life by discovering your purpose, envisioning your future, and writing your personal vision and mission statement.

Truly effective leaders are those who have figured out what is important to them, what matters in their life and what they stand for. They have identified their purpose and are living it daily. You must passionately pursue your purpose in life and relentlessly challenge yourself to become better. Few things are more important than a vision for your life and a mission statement to achieve your vision.

Be transformed by the renewing of your heart, mind, body and soul

Deliberate development, training, and education helps you to develop comprehensive and wide-ranging thinking and problem-solving skills that enable you to state and define problems in a volatile, uncertain, complex, and ambiguous atmosphere. It can provide you with a breadth and depth of knowledge and critical thinking skill that will help you to think of not only the first order of effect of a decision but the second, of third, and fourth order of effect of your decisions.

Every day look for ways to renew yourself and build resiliency into your life. Go to the gym or for a walk to strengthen your body. Read a book or take a class to keep your mind focused and thoughtful. Go to your favorite place to worship to renew your souls. Spend time with family and friends to fortify the love in your heart. Finally, energy and enthusiasm are two of the necessary qualities a leader needs to survive and thrive. By renewing yourself you stay energetic and enthusiastic.

Forget the past and move toward the future

Learn from your past mistakes and your past successes but don't try to relive them. Progress is about moving forward in your life, career and leadership. Holding onto the past will hold you back from future achievements. By forgetting what is behind you and driving toward the future you will continue to grow, develop and reinvent yourself.

Teach others

Take time to teach others how to find their purpose and share a piece of your life with them. The best way to learn something is to teach it to another person. It is also the best way to let other people know that you care about their development and are interested in their growth.

Encouragement and Grace

A leader is an agent of hope. Your people want to become the very best they can and through you leadership they will. Provide encouragement as they grow and develop it will lift them up and provide the confidence to continue.

Bestow Grace when they make mistakes. It is very easy to yell and get angry over mistakes but by doing so you miss an opportunity to continue to develop the person. Show them the error of their ways but reinforce the correct way to do the task or job.

Be a Servant Leader

I believe we are hard wired to connect and serve with one another. If we were not hard wired to connect then social media would not have lasted as long as it has. We need to communicate and connect with one another. Serving one another is an outcropping of our leadership and how we develop others.

Final thought

Don't sell yourself short, you only get one chance to make a difference and an impact. Take the time and envision where you want to be 5,10, an 20 years from now then put your plan in to action and achieve your dream!

Leaving a Legacy

Each of us will face a time when we are concerned about what legacy we will leave to our children, grandchildren, and our future generations. This book is my way of passing on some wisdom and insight to my children, grandchildren, and their children.

The ideas and concepts in this book represent how I have grown, developed, and reinvented myself on a daily basis. I cannot live their lives, but I can pass on what I have learned so they do not have to make the same mistakes and they can learn from my journey.

Their choices will determine their destiny. Their choices will determine if they live unstoppable lives.

King Solomon passed on some sage advice to his sons that I believe is still relevant today. His proverb is solid advice and can be passed on. In addition, when they grow older, they can teach their own children.

My children, listen to what your father teaches you. Pay attention, and you will have understanding. What I am teaching you is good, so remember it all. When I was only a little boy, my parents' son, my father would teach me. He would say, "Remember what I say and never forget it. Do as I tell you, and you will live. Get wisdom and insight! Do not forget or ignore what I say. Do not abandon wisdom, and she will protect you; love her, and she will keep you safe. Getting wisdom is the most important thing you can do. Whatever else you get, get insight. Love wisdom, and she will make you great. Embrace her, and she will bring you honor. She will be your crowning glory."

Listen to me, my child. Take seriously, what I am telling you, and you will live a long life. I have taught you wisdom and the right way to live. Nothing will stand in your way if you walk wisely, and you will not stumble when you run. Always remember what you have learned. Your education is your life—guard it well.

Do not go where evil people go. Do not follow the example of the wicked. Don't do it! Keep away from evil! Refuse it and go on your way. Wicked people cannot sleep unless they have done something wrong. They lie awake unless they have hurt someone. Evil and violence are like food and drink to them.

The road the wise travel is like the sunrise, getting brighter and brighter until daylight has come. The road of the wicked, however, is dark as night. They fall, but cannot see what they have stumbled over.My child, pay attention to what I say. Listen to my words. Never let them get away from you. Remember them and keep them in your heart. They will give life and health to anyone who understands them.

Be careful how you think; your life is shaped by your thoughts. Never say anything that is not true. Have nothing to do with lies and misleading words. Look straight ahead with honest confidence; do not hang your head in shame. Plan carefully what you do, and whatever you do will turn out right. Avoid evil and walk straight ahead. Do not go one step off the right way.

Your Unstoppable legacy needs to be passed on to your future generations. It is your responsibility to let those who come after you to know what you stood for, what was important in your life, and why your choose the life your led. King Solomon's advice is good even today.

History tells us that life is not perfect, easy, equal, or fair. Life is life. It is up to you to develop, grow, and reinvent yourself every day to meet the challenges of this world. Take a stand for your beliefs and fight back instead of compromising. Always have Faith in God.

It begins with FAITH! All you need is the faith as small as a grain of a mustard seed to begin. Faith is the inner strength that gives you the outer strength you need to rise above the status quo.

Faith strengthens your belief in yourself and fortifies you for the challenges and risks you will face. Faith reminds you that when everything around you is in chaos, you can turn to your faith to find a way through it all. It begins with a belief in who you are.

Then, watch it grow as you believe in yourself, your capabilities, and your unstoppable life. Let God be your guide and compass along the way and your life will be unstoppable. God, who formed you and placed you on this earth to serve a purpose, would not have designed you to be inadequate for your purpose.

Consequently, if God created and shaped you for a purpose, He will give you the strength you need to push forward when the road challenges. Your faith in yourself, your faith in your abilities and talents will carry you along to the finish line.

- You need an unyielding faith that you are here for a purpose, that your life has meaning, and that your life is a gift.
- You need an undying belief in yourself and your purpose in life.
- You need an unwavering faith in your skills, abilities, capabilities, and talents.

You need faith that you can change your life. Never stop having faith in yourself and keep your eye on the prize!

Live L.I.F.E on Mission!

When do you begin?

Begin **NOW** changing your thoughts

Begin **NOW** living authentically

Begin **NOW** believing in yourself

Begin **NOW** Living your Life

Begin **NOW** taking control of your life

Begin **NOW** letting love shine through

Begin **NOW** letting your voice be heard

Begin **NOW** being true to yourself

Begin **NOW** living congruently

Begin **NOW** envision your future

Begin **NOW** it is your Time!

NOW LIVE your **UNSTOPPABLE LIFE!**

ABOUT THE AUTHOR

Thomas S. Narofsky is the Founder and Chief Inspirational Officer for the Narofsky Consulting Group, a leadership development, team effectiveness, and executive coaching consultancy. He is the developer of the F(X) Leadership Model, the Unstoppable Model, and the Inspire or Retire Leadership Theorem and author of *F(X) Leadership Unleashed!*

Thom retired in November 2011 as the Command Senior Enlisted Leader for United States Strategic Command after serving 28 years on active duty in the United States Air Force. In his capacity as a Combatant Command Senior Enlisted Leader, he served on the Department of Defense Senior Enlisted Leader Council, the United States Strategic Command Joint Enlisted Development Council, and the United States Air Force Enlisted Board of Directors. He has conducted worldwide professional and leadership development seminars with U.S, Korean, Japanese, Australian, British, Canadian, Belgian, and German enlisted forces. His military decorations include Defense Superior Service Medal and the Bronze Star.

Thom is an adjunct professor at Bellevue University in the Arts and Sciences Department. He holds a Master of Arts in Leadership, a Master of Science in Information Technology Management, a Bachelor of Science in Interdisciplinary Studies, and two associates degrees. He received Executive Leadership Development Certificates from the Center for Creative Leadership, University of North Carolina at Chapel Hill and the University of Tennessee